Frank Lloyd Wright
& the Prairie School in Wisconsin

An Architectural Touring Guide

Kristin Visser

PRAIRIE OAK PRESS
Madison, Wisconsin

First edition, first printing
Copyright © 1992 by Kristin Visser

Prairie Oak Press
2577 University Avenue
Madison, Wisconsin 53705

Designed and produced by Flying Fish Graphics, Blue Mounds, Wisconsin
Printed in the United States of America by Braun-Brumfield, Inc., Ann Arbor, Michigan

Library of Congress Cataloging-in-Publication Data

Visser, Kristin, 1949-
    Frank Lloyd Wright and the Prairie School in Wisconsin: an architectural touring guide by Kristin Visser. — 1st ed.
        p.   cm.
        ISBN 1-879483-07-6: $24.95 — ISBN 1-879483-08-4 (pbk.) $16.95
        1. Prairie school (Architecture)—Wisconsin—Guidebooks.
2. Architecture, Modern—20th century—Wisconsin—Guidebooks.
3. Wright, Frank Lloyd, 1867-1959—Themes, motives. I. Title.
NA730.W5V57   1992
720'.9775'0904—dc20   92-5217
                                            CIP

Contents

Cover photo: Unitarian Meeting House, Madison. Frank Lloyd Wright.
Photo by Kristin Visser. All photos by author unless otherwise indicated.

Introduction

When Frank Lloyd Wright died in the spring of 1959, two months short of his ninety-second birthday, much of the significant literature on his life and career had been written by the architect himself. The primary source on the subject was his *An Autobiography*. To add to his numerous shorter writings, Horizon Press published his beautifully designed and illustrated series of testaments during the 1950s, including *The Natural House*. The two major scholarly surveys of his architecture were Henry-Russell Hitchcock's *In the Nature of Materials: The Buildings of Frank Lloyd Wright, 1887-1941* and Grant Manson's *Frank Lloyd Wright to 1910: The First Golden Age*, which one could carry around Chicago, especially Oak Park, in hopes of locating some of the houses illustrated. There was no such thing as a Wright guidebook let alone one to the Chicago Prairie School that the young genius from Wisconsin had begun to influence by the mid-to-late 1890s.

As an out-of-state graduate student at the University of Wisconsin-Madison from 1957 through 1961, I was fortunate enough to have a native guide. Dave Healy, a fellow student who remains a close friend and colleague in the History Department at the University of Wisconsin-Milwaukee, would take me on fast-paced architectural walks around Madison. While we had no trouble tracking down the Wright houses, and we visited his Unitarian Meeting House on the western edge of the campus many times, we could only guess, if we ever tried, at which architects had designed the houses recognizably Prairie School in style. And that was the case even with Madison's premier example: the large Bradley/Sigma Phi fraternity house in University Heights. Was it really a Louis Sullivan design, or was it by George Elmslie? We needed a reliably accurate and portable reference to tell us.

Since the early 1960s the literature on Frank Lloyd Wright's architecture has expanded at an accelerated rate. Several biographies have been published, the most scholarly being that of Robert Twombly, whose interpretive study began as a Ph.D. dissertation for the University of Wisconsin-Madison history department and reappeared in its final, revised edition in the late 1970s. During the following decade, the Frank Lloyd Wright Archives, under the direction of Bruce Brooks Pfeiffer at Taliesin West, caught up with the growing demand for increased availability of sources. It not only made available its holdings to researchers but published three volumes of Wright letters and generated four oversized volumes of Wright drawings. The latter complete a set of twelve monographs published by A.D.A. EDITA, Tokyo, which includes a running text by Pfeiffer. Photographs, many in color, of more than eight hundred existing Wright buildings fill the first eight of its chronologically-arranged volumes. All the photography is by the owner-editor of the publishing house, the master architectural photographer Yukio Futagawa. He has followed up with another picture-book series, *Selected Houses by Wright*, in eight slightly smaller volumes, again with a text by Pfeiffer.

There is hardly a coffee table designed to accommodate such a sumptuous pictorial display. Moreover, the size, quality, and arrangement of any one of the Futagawa volumes would preclude its serving as a handy field book for touring Frank Lloyd Wright buildings. This purpose has been served in its most comprehensive form by the well-known guide compiled by William Storrer in the early 1970s and revised in 1978, *The Architecture of Frank Lloyd Wright: A Complete Catalog.* Indexed by Zip Codes as well as alphabet, it is also complete with addresses, if no final directions on how to find them. This shortcoming aside, a Wright buff crossing a state line in search of another example can hardly do without it. By now, however, it is out of date. As a result of changing conditions, most happily through restorations, many of the houses are in need of new and expanded descriptions and, more important, new photographs.

With regard to Prairie School architecture, its vast assortment of practitioners and wide distribution of coinciding examples would doubtless discourage anyone from compiling a comprehensive guidebook on the subject. The most useful general publication on the subject remains the well-illustrated 1972 book by H. Allen Brooks, *The Prairie School: Frank Lloyd Wright and His Midwest Contemporaries.*

Among states blessed with a rich assortment of Wright architecture, at least the top four—Illinois, California, Michigan, and Wisconsin—deserve their own, specialized Wright guidebooks. For Illinois, University of Wisconsin-Milwaukee architectural historian Paul Sprague published a concise and well-illustrated guide in 1976 for touring Prairie School as well as Wright designs in Oak Park (leaving the rest of greater Chicago and the state at large for someone else to do). The Wright buildings in California were treated in an oversized book of glossy color photographs in the late 1980s, including an overview preface and brief descriptions by architectural historian David Gebhard, the co-author of a guide to Los Angeles architecture in general. Michigan has recently acquired a reference book to its Frank Lloyd Wright houses written by A. Dale Northrup, but still lacks a guidebook to aid in touring them.

The first genuine guidebook that concentrates exclusively on a single state's Frank Lloyd Wright buildings is the one in your hand. As Paul Sprague did for Oak Park, Kristin Visser implies an art historical context for the featured subject of Wright by including major Prairie School examples designed by Chicago-trained architects for Wisconsin patrons. Whether by Wisconsin's own or by one of the various contemporaries he managed to outlive and aesthetically outdistance, each existing work is personalized through a discussion of its patronage, identified with the stylistic traits of its architect, and directly described in discrete detail. Original articulation of interior and exterior spaces, condition, restoration or rehabilitation, and changes in the function of a building are also discussed as vital to its history and present character. The "Also of Interest" sections of the book lead to further architectural adventures.

This wealth of information is preceded by a biographical sketch of Wright, a concise discussion of the origins and evolution of the Prairie School, and biographical notes on its architects active in Wisconsin. If momentarily thumbed through, the survey of more than one hundred photographs alone presents a lasting impression of the most creative aspect of the state's architecture. In hand, on tour, this detailed field guide serves either the casual fan or the avid aficionado of this beautiful legacy incomparably well.

James M. Dennis
Usonia I, Madison, Wisconsin
March 10, 1992

Foreword

Wisconsin is home to some of the world's greatest architecture. More than forty of Frank Lloyd Wright's buildings, spanning his entire career, are found here. In addition, dozens of Wisconsin buildings designed by other architects of the Prairie School have long been recognized as important works in their own right. A guide including the work of other important Prairie School architects, along with that of Wright, allows the reader a more complete picture of the growth and development of the Prairie School, of which Wright was the initiator and chief proponent. His work, along with that of the other architects represented in this book, left a permanent mark on the architecture not only of Wisconsin and the Midwest, but of all American and European building from the turn of the century to the present.

Despite this rich trove of Wisconsin architecture, there was until now no comprehensive guide to the buildings of Wright and his early 20th-century contemporaries. I have tried to provide a dependable and easy-to-use guide for anyone with an interest in Wright, the Prairie School, and Wisconsin's unique architectural heritage.

This book includes an introduction to Wright and the Prairie School, followed by descriptions and photos of some eighty buildings—all Wright's Wisconsin buildings, and nearly forty of the most important Prairie School buildings in the state. In addition, I include information on access to buildings open to the public, historic walking tours, other buildings of interest, and sources of travel information. To make visiting the buildings as convenient as possible, they are listed geographically, rather than by architect. In each community, buildings are also listed in an order that makes for convenient visiting. (A chronological list of buildings by architect is included as an appendix.)

Though the book includes much information gleaned from interviews with owners of buildings, it is not a scholarly work. My sources of information include publications about Wright and the Prairie school, several masters' theses, files of the State Historical Society of Wisconsin and local landmarks commissions, interviews, and my own observations in visiting the buildings.

The dates used in the book refer to the years in which the buildings were designed, or in some cases the dates of the building permits. In most cases, construction began in the same year, or the year following. In some situations, construction was delayed for several years. Those cases are noted in the discussion about the buildings.

I will appreciate communications from readers concerning any inaccuracies that might have found their way into the book (and for which I take full responsibility), as well as other Prairie School buildings that might be included in a future edition.

Many of the buildings in this book are private residences not open to the public. Please respect the privacy and property of the residents.

Acknowledgments

This book is the result of nearly two years of research, travel, and interviews. Though I am the sole author, and therefore to blame for any mistakes, the book could not have been completed without the help of many people.

Special thanks go to Tim Heggland, who provided invaluable assistance and encouragement throughout the project. Without him, I'd still be buried in a pile of historic structure surveys in the basement of the State Historical Library.

Professor Jim Dennis was especially helpful early on in the project, not only in giving me a tour of his Wright-designed home but in helping me find sources of information about other buildings in the Madison area. Pat Ivory of the Eau Claire Landmarks Commission, John Florine of the La Crosse City Planning Department, and Katherine Rankin of the Madison City Planning Department assisted me in finding information about the buildings in those cities, and Don Aucutt provided considerable information about buildings in Wausau, as well as a tour of his Wright-designed home. Stan Mallach of the Milwaukee Area Research Center of the State Historical Society of Wisconsin provided invaluable information about the work of Russell Barr Williamson.

Thanks also to Dixie Legler and to Tom Casey of the Taliesin Fellowship, who gave me a fascinating tour of the Taliesin complex. Jon Vondracek and Richard Kinch of the Johnson Foundation were equally kind in showing me Wingspread, as was Nancy Kind, of the Farmers and Merchants Union Bank, who gave me a tour and patiently answered my questions. And Harvey Glanzer, owner of the A.D. German Warehouse, took me on a tour and explained his plans for that unique building. Audrey Laatsch of the Seth Peterson Cottage Conservancy provided helpful suggestions about whom to interview.

The librarians in Barron, Evansville, Merrill, Reedsburg, Tomah, and Wisconsin Dells helped me find local history materials that proved invaluable in writing the sections on the Claude and Starck libraries.

Thanks to the staff of the Visual and Sound Archives of the State Historical Society of Wisconsin. They were unendingly patient and helpful during my search for historic photos.

A special note of appreciation to Jerry Minnich, who suggested several years ago that if I was interested in Wright, I should write a book.

Finally, my thanks and unending gratitude to the owners of the homes listed in this book who graciously allowed me to visit them and who willingly submitted to inverviews: Edith Anderson, Julie and Clarke Arnold, David and Jill Arena, Todd Barry and Margaret Lewis, Chris and Vickie Born, Jackie Boynton, John and Cindy Edwards, John and Barbara Ferry, Patricia Fleming, Pam Frautschi and James Boudreau, Elsie Gabrielsen, Jim Gourley, Stuart and Cleone Hawkinson, Eileen Immerman, Pat and Margaret Kinney, Karen Kling, Karen and John Kraus, David and Joanne Litzow, Norma Marz, Scott McDonald, Craig and Nancy Miller, Barb Pratzel, Robert and Joyce Voight, Sylvia Weathers, and Michael Wissell. Without their help and cooperation, this book could not have been written.

Frank Lloyd Wright

In a 1991 survey, members of the American Institute of Architects (AIA) recognized Frank Lloyd Wright as the greatest American architect of all time. In that same survey, Fallingwater, Wright's amazing weekend retreat for a client in western Pennsylvania, was chosen the best work ever by an American architect.

Consider Wright's impact on American (not to mention European) architecture, and try to imagine how this country would look had Wright not existed. Among his innovations are the open-plan house with no attic or basement (from which the ranch house is a direct descendent) and the carport. Imagine suburbs without those staples. Wright was a pioneer in the use of air conditioning, in fireproof construction, in passive solar design, in the use of indirect lighting, and in the use of plate glass, plywood, reinforced concrete, and other new materials. One of his last (unbuilt) designs was for a multi-story, big-city hotel with a huge open atrium in the center.

Through a remarkable career spanning more than seventy years, more than four hundred buildings from his designs were built, while hundreds of other designs were completed on paper, but never executed. So modern and appealing are his buildings that even more than thirty years after his death, unbuilt designs are still being hauled out of the Taliesin archives and built.

Wright's career began with designs for Queen Anne and Shingle style buildings—the sort that home-owners and builders of the late 19th century expected. By 1900 his Prairie houses had begun to open up the plan of the house, with living and dining spaces flowing together, frequently around a central fireplace, and lots of glass in rows of windows and in doors to minimize the difference between indoors and outdoors. In the 1920s, he began laying out floor plans in grids. The next step was

Frank Lloyd Wright Archives

Wright as a young man about 1887

State Historical Society of Wisconsin

Wright, about 1924

the Usonian house of the 1930s, in which the basement and attic disappeared and the fireplace, kitchen, bathroom, and utility room were clustered in a service core. About 1940, Wright got tired of right angles and began designing houses as semi-circles, or on hexagonal or diamond grids. By the time he died he was working with circles, spirals and ellipses.

Though most of his practice was residential, Wright designed office buildings, churches, theaters, museums, hotels, warehouses, schools, government centers, a university campus, restaurants, medical clinics, even service stations. (He was a lover of the automobile and a tireless campaigner to have Americans come to grips with the

2

decentralizing effects of the automobile—and to plan for those effects.)

Wright was a total artist. Not only did he design buildings, he designed the furniture to go in them. He also designed rugs, upholstery fabrics, light fixtures and lamps, urns and vases, leaded glass windows, and complete sets of dishes along with matching serving pieces and silverware. He designed murals and sculptures. He created decorative panels of terra cotta, wood, plaster, metal, even concrete. He designed dresses for his first wife and for the wives of some early clients. In his view, even the clothes worn in his houses should be part of a grand design.

Frank Lloyd Wright was born in Richland Center, Wisconsin, on June 8, 1867. (He insisted for years that he was born in 1869, but, along with many fabrications about his life that he persisted in repeating, the 1869 birth date has been proven to be wrong.) His mother was Anna Lloyd Jones, a teacher and a member of a large Welsh family that came to Wisconsin and by the mid-1850s had settled just outside the tiny Wisconsin River community of Spring Green. The brothers, sisters, aunts and uncles, cousins, and other relatives eventually owned the entire valley.

Wright's father William Russell Cary Wright was an itinerant preacher, music teacher, lawyer, and orator from Massachusetts. He ended up in Lone Rock, near Spring Green, a widower with three children. (After he married Anna in 1866, the children from the first marriage were shipped off to live with William Wright's relatives, apparently because of Anna's inability to get along with them.)

Frank Lloyd Wright was born while William was a preacher in the Richland Center area. Two sisters, Jane and Maginel, were born 1869 and 1877. The family moved several times while Frank was young—to Iowa, Rhode Island, Massachusetts—before returning to Wisconsin and settling in Madison in 1878, where William worked as pastor of the Unitarian church. To supplement his income, he gave music lessons, preached at other churches, and gave lectures. Young Frank attended school and worked summers on the Lloyd Jones farms.

In 1885, William and Anna Wright divorced. William left, and Frank never saw his father again. Frank was forced to work to help support his mother and two sisters. He got a job in the architectural office of Allan Conover, who was also a professor of engineering at the University of Wisconsin (see p. 95).

In early 1887, after nearly two years with Conover and two semesters as a "special student" at the university, Wright left Madison and moved to Chicago. He landed a job in the office of Joseph Lyman Silsbee, with whom he had connections through his uncle Jenkin Lloyd Jones (see Unity Chapel, p. 179). Wright worked for Silsbee about a year, during which time he received his first independent commission

3

—buildings for the progressive Hillside School his aunts Nell and Jane Lloyd Jones operated at Spring Green.

Silsbee was a progressive architect and an important influence on Wright. Not only did Wright continue to learn about architecture in Silsbee's office, he began to meet other young architects, including George Maher and George Elmslie, who also worked in the office.

Sometime in early 1888, Wright left Silsbee and went to work as a draftsman for the firm owned by Dankmar Adler and Louis Sullivan. For six years, Wright worked closely with Louis Sullivan, and Sullivan is the only source to whom Wright ever acknowledged a direct debt. (The debt was deep and long lasting. In Sullivan's declining years, when he was beset by personal and financial troubles, and no commissions were coming in, Wright regularly sent him money.)

While working for Sullivan, Wright designed several residential commissions that came to the firm. Since Adler and Sullivan both preferred to work on larger offices and commercial structures, they turned over smaller commissions such as houses to their young associates.

During this time, Wright married Catherine Tobin and moved to Oak Park, where the young couple built a house. They eventually had six children. Wright also began moonlighting—accepting independent commissions from neighbors and friends —while still working for Sullivan. According to Wright, he left Sullivan's employ in 1893 because his moonlighting was found out and he was asked to leave.

Wright opened an office in Chicago, and in 1895 built a studio attached to his Oak Park home. Though he did most of his design work in Oak Park, Wright kept an office in downtown Chicago as a place to meet with clients, and perhaps also because in the same building were the offices of several other progressive young architects, including Robert Spencer, Jr., and Walter Burley Griffin, whom Wright would soon hire to work in his Oak Park studio. Griffin became one of Wright's chief assistants and went on to a long career in Australia.

Wright was also a member of "The Eighteen," a group of architects who met regularly to discuss ideas and projects. This contact with his peers, several of whom would become leaders of the Prairie movement, was critical in the formation of many of Wright's ideas about architecture.

Historians consider either the Harley Bradley house (1900) in Kankakee, Illinois, or the Ward Willits house (1901) in Highland Park, Illinois, to be Wright's first realized Prairie School building. From 1895 until 1909, Wright's fame and influence spread steadily. He was a tireless lecturer and writer, and published a number of articles and house plans in both architectural journals and in popular ladies' home-decorating

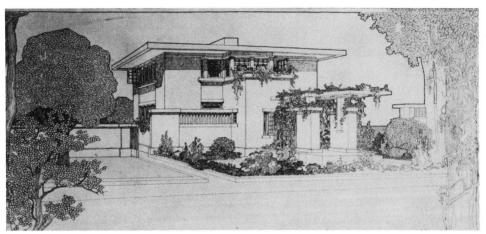

State Historical Society of Wisconsin

"A Fireproof House for $5,000"

magazines. Particularly influential were plans published in the *Ladies Home Journal* in 1901, and in April, 1907. His 1907 "Fireproof House for $5000" was the basis of many designs by other architects, as well as homes Wright himself designed.

Wright was at the height of his career, just over forty years old, with a thriving architectural practice employing a number of talented assistants, socially prominent in Oak Park, with a devoted wife and six children, when he abruptly turned his practice over to another architect and left for Europe with Mamah Borthwick Cheney, the wife of an Oak Park client.

They spent nearly a year in Europe, while Wright prepared an edition of his building plans for publication in Germany. (He was then more famous in Europe than in America.) When they returned, Wright found it impossible to return to his studio, so he and Mamah left Oak Park for Spring Green and Taliesin, the home Wright was building for them on Lloyd Jones land his mother had given him (see p. 159).

Scandal followed the couple, and even though Mamah soon obtained a divorce, Catherine would not divorce Wright. The scandal caused the loss of some clients, but Wright kept others, and maintained offices at Taliesin and in Chicago, where he employed a number of assistants, including Russell Barr Williamson.

In August, 1914, Mamah, her two children, and four others were brutally murdered at Taliesin by a deranged servant who barricaded them in the dining room and set the building on fire. Those who managed to escape the flames he killed with an ax as they ran from the burning building.

Wright was in Chicago working on a major commission when he heard the news. He and Mamah's ex-husband rushed together to Taliesin. Mr. Cheney left with the bodies of his two children. Wright buried Mamah in the family cemetery at Unity Chapel.

The next two decades of Wright's life were especially difficult. He rebuilt Taliesin, but spent much of the time from 1917 through 1922 in Japan working on the Imperial Hotel, one of his largest and most famous commissions. With him was Miriam Noel, who had befriended him after Mamah's murder. After finally obtaining a divorce from Catherine, Wright married Miriam in November, 1923.

Miriam proved to be unstable and difficult. After more than six years with him before marriage, they split up within five months of being married. For the next few years, Miriam hounded Wright for money, especially after he met and began living with Olgivanna Milanov Hinzenberg, a 26-year-old divorcee with a small child. She and Wright had a daughter, Iovanna, in late 1925. The popular press had a field day with Wright's newest domestic scandal (which included hiding out in Minnesota, being arrested for allegedly taking Olgivanna across state lines for immoral purposes, and spending the night in jail). After finally securing a divorce from Miriam, Wright married Olgivanna in August, 1928.

While his personal troubles mounted, so did his professional ones. Part of Taliesin II burned in 1925, the result of a fire started by faulty wiring. Wright had only a few remaining clients, mainly in California, and he owed back taxes and other debts. To prevent him from losing Taliesin, in 1927 several friends organized "Wright, Incorporated" and sold shares of stock to raise money to help him gain control of his finances and pay his debts.

By the late 1920s and early 1930s, Wright was viewed by most architects and historians as an important figure, but a retired one. He was justly famous for his Prairie houses, for Unity Temple in Oak Park, and for other buildings around the country. But his California houses inspired little favorable comment, he was over 60, and he had completed no major works since the Imperial Hotel in 1922. He was forced to make a living lecturing and writing. And write he did. He produced dozens of articles and books during this period, including his autobiography.

He and Olgivanna began the Taliesin Fellowship in 1932, probably as much in response to financial pressure as anything else; they could use the tuition money and the essentially free help to run Taliesin at a time during the Depression when clients were especially scarce. The Fellowship proved to be smashingly successful. The apprentices began by remodeling Hillside School and other buildings on the Taliesin grounds, since there were still few commissions.

Frank and Olgivanna
Wright in the late
1930s

State Historical Society of Wisconsin.

Then came 1936. Commissions for three of Wright's most famous and important buildings came all at once. Edgar Kaufman, millionaire owner of a Pittsburgh department store and father of a Taliesin apprentice, requested a design for a weekend retreat in the mountains of western Pennsylvania. Herbert Jacobs, a Madison newspaper reporter, asked Wright to design an inexpensive but functional and efficient home (see p. 121). And Herbert Johnson asked Wright if he would care to submit a design for a new administration building for S.C. Johnson and Son in Racine (see p. 19).

The amazing Wright, age 69, embarked on his second career. Between 1936 and his death in 1959, he designed hundreds of buildings, of which more than two hundred were actually constructed. Wright had spent winters in Arizona periodically since the late 1920s, and in 1937 he and the Fellowship created Taliesin West outside Scottsdale, which Wright intended to be a permanent winter home. (Because of pneumonia and other health problems, doctors had suggested that Wright spend winters in a warmer, dryer climate than Spring Green offered.)

Because of his tremendous outpouring of creative designs in the 1930s, 1940s, and 1950s, and also because of his continuing, and sometimes shameless, self-promotion, Wright was the most famous architect in the world at the time of his death.

He never achieved the same heights of popularity at home in Wisconsin, however. He constantly owed money to local merchants. He periodically made insulting remarks about various communities in Wisconsin and various buildings in those communities (though he happily insulted communities and buildings everywhere, not just Wisconsin). He had what many considered to be suspect political beliefs; he was a pacifist during World War II, and he professed admiration for some aspects of Soviet society. By the end of his life, though, Wisconsin had begun to recognize Wright's genius with an honorary degree from the University of Wisconsin, testimonials, and commissions from Wisconsin residents. (He really wanted official recognition through government commissions, which he never received. His only government building in Wisconsin is the Wyoming Valley School—see p. 183.)

Wright died in Scottsdale on April 9, 1959, at age 91, a few days after surgery for an intestinal blockage. The next day, William Wesley Peters, who had been the Taliesin Fellowship's first apprentice in 1932, and who was by 1959 Wright's second in command, put Wright's embalmed and coffined body in a truck and drove day and night to Spring Green. There, Olgivanna, Peters, and other Fellowship members had a simple funeral ceremony presided over by the pastor of the Madison Unitarian Meeting House. Wright was buried near Mamah Cheney in the family cemetery next to Unity Chapel. On his metal grave marker were the words "Love of an Idea is Love of God."

Olgivanna continued to run the Fellowship. When she died in 1985, her will stated that Wright's body should be exhumed and removed to Taliesin West, there to be cremated and his ashes mingled with hers. (Olgivanna didn't like Wisconsin because she was treated badly in her early, and unmarried, years with Wright. Some historians also speculate that she was jealous of Mamah Cheney.) Though Wright had clearly wanted to be buried in Wisconsin, Fellowship members followed Olgivanna's wishes and Wright's remains now lie in Arizona. His original gravestone at Unity Chapel remains as a monument.

Decades after his death, Wright is, if anything, more famous today than when he was alive. What prompts this continuing fascination? Perhaps it is because Wright's buildings are timeless. They are as interesting, as comfortable, and as inviting today as they were when they were built.

Wright was most certainly a genius. He lived in a time of great changes in technology, in society, in values. He was able to fuse brilliantly many different artistic, technical and social elements—the Arts and Crafts movement, Japanese art and architecture, Mayan architecture, the advent of the automobile, changes in family life brought about by the introduction of labor-saving appliances—into his own unique designs. He loved new technologies and embraced plywood, reinforced concrete, and other new materials immediately. He had the ability to imagine in three dimensions—to walk through a building in his mind before putting plans down on paper. And he was a master at tying a building, its site, and its furnishings together into a coherent and pleasing—an organic—whole.

He was also a master at manipulating space and light. His buildings are infinitely interesting. The play of different ceiling heights, different corridor widths, long vistas, careful placement of windows to catch the changing light and shadow as the sun moves through the sky, the careful planning down to the smallest details of ornament make Wright's buildings endlessly fascinating and enjoyable to be in.

Wright spent his entire career working toward "the destruction of the box." By that he meant not only opening up the floor plan by eliminating the boxy rooms found in Victorian homes, but also eliminating traditional corner supporting posts and opening up the house to the outside with French doors and lots of windows.

Wright designed buildings he called "organic," that is, buildings that use natural materials, such as stone, wood, and brick, that are appropriate to the climate and to the site, and, most important, are designed to meet the needs of the occupants.

Louis Sullivan said, "Form follows function." Wright said, "Form and function are one."

State Historical Society of Wisconsin

Wright at his 87th birthday party, June 8, 1956

The Prairie School

The late 19th century was a time of massive social change in the United States. The population was growing rapidly. The economy was changing from agricultural to industrial, with the concomitant growth of cities. An urban middle class was forming, and moving to the suburbs, which were a new phenomenon created by the development of streetcars, trolleys and other mass transit. Labor-saving devices, electricity, steam heat, and other innovations were changing the American home. Women increasingly had opportunities for work in factories and offices, giving them options beyond domestic service. The number of servants declined precipitously. After the Civil War, and as the United States became a world power, Americans increasingly withdrew from European influence and began to search for things uniquely American—whether in our character, in our business and social activities, or in architecture and art.

In the late 19th century, several trends in art and architecture emerged. Architects, social commentators, and home decorating magazines led a rebellion against the cluttered and fussy Victorian housing styles of the period. The search for a uniquely American architecture, one not associated with the historical European styles, had begun with H.H. Richardson and other architects on the east coast, and spread to Chicago, where Louis Sullivan led the development of the "Chicago School" of commercial architecture. The Arts and Crafts movement, which began in England, had as its premise the search for simplicity and naturalness in homes, furnishings, and decorative items. Chicago became the center of the Arts and Crafts movement in the United States.

Architects and magazine writers expounded on the virtues of less elaborate homes (no more turrets, towers, and gewgaws) made of natural materials like wood, brick, and stone. They wanted more open floor plans, with multi-purpose rooms that could be used for entertaining, reading, and family gatherings. They wanted simpler, lighter furnishings—no more heavy tables and dark cabinets cluttered with knickknacks and surrounded by the forests of potted palms found in Victorian parlors.

One housing style that satisfied this need was the bungalow, which had roots in India, the Arts and Crafts movement, and other sources. By the turn of the century, Americans had adopted the bungalow, especially on the west coast. The American foursquare, a solid, square, two-story home with minimum decoration, was another answer to the desire for a simple, uncluttered, open-plan home. Foursquare homes and bungalows were very popular in the Midwest.

Frank Lloyd Wright and his circle took the popular design concepts of the day and created something unique and original in the application of those concepts. Prairie architects wanted to create a wholly American architecture, one distinct from that of Europe. Purcell and Elmslie, writing in 1913, said, "The dynamics of Greek Architecture was a purely personal matter with the Greek—it belongs to him, and he—he is long since dead; so is the Roman dead and so is the medieval romanticist dead. Why should we have the cerements of by-gone architecture habiting our new problems, our fresh, vital, instinctive Architectural work?"

Writing in his autobiography, Wright explains how he solved those purely American problems with the creation of the Prairie house, "My first feeling therefore had been a yearning for simplicity. A new sense of simplicity as 'organic'....I loved the prairie by instinct as a great simplicity...I saw that a little height on the prairie was enough to look like much more...I had an idea that the horizontal planes in buildings, those planes parallel to earth, identify themselves with the ground—make the building belong to the ground....

"First thing in building the new house, get rid of the attic...get rid of the unwholesome basement...Instead of lean, brick chimneys bristling up everywhere...I could see necessity for one chimney only. A broad generous one, or at most two. These kept low-down on gently sloping roofs or perhaps flat roofs....Taking a human being for my scale, I brought the whole house down in height to fit a normal one—ergo, 5'8 1/2" tall [Wright's height], say....My sense of 'wall' was no longer the side of a box. It was enclosure of space affording protection against storm or heat only when needed. But it was also to bring the outside world into the house and let the inside of the house go outside. In this sense, I was working away at the wall as a wall and bringing it towards the function of a screen, a means of opening up space...I gave the broad protecting roof-shelter to the whole...The house began to associate with the ground and become natural to its prairie site....

"Dwellings of that period were cut up....The interiors consisted of boxes beside boxes or inside boxes, called rooms....I could see little sense in this...So I declared the whole lower floor as one room...Then I screened various portions of the big room for certain domestic purposes like dining, reading, receiving callers....Thus came an end to the cluttered house. Fewer doors; fewer window holes though much greater window area; windows and doors lowered to convenient human heights." (Frank Lloyd Wright, *An Autobiography*, Duell, Sloan and Pearce, 1943.)

Wright's first Prairie houses were built in 1900 and 1901 in the Chicago suburbs. From the turn of the century until the end of World War I, Prairie architects turned out thousands of Prairie houses, primarily in the Midwest, but also in California, Utah, upstate New York, Florida, Texas, even as far away as Puerto Rico. Though their work was primarily residential, they modified the style to create Prairie banks, churches, schools, offices, libraries, government buildings, and commercial structures.

It's difficult to easily define any style, especially one that had a dozen or more creative architects working in it, but in general Prairie style buildings are characterized by: open interiors, usually with a focus on a large central fireplace in the residential buildings; furniture, light fixtures, murals and other decorations designed specifically to be a part of each building; sparing use of decorative elements; emphasis on the horizontal, especially the use of low or flat roofs with wide overhangs, rows of windows, and bands of decorative trim; use of simple, geometric shapes, and sharp, clean-cut edges and corners; melding inside and outside through lots of windows and glass doors. Finally, Prairie buildings use natural materials, especially wood, brick, stone, stucco and plaster, as they appear in their natural state, i.e. wood is not painted, rather it is stained or oiled to allow the grain to be seen.

By 1918, Americans began turning back to historical revival buildings, especially Tudor, Georgian and Colonial style homes and commercial structures. There are several reasons for this abandonment of the Prairie style. Wright, its creator and chief proponent, moved on to a new phase in his work and quit designing Prairie buildings. Professional architectural journals dropped coverage of Prairie architecture in favor of the revival styles. The eastern architectural establishment had never embraced the Prairie School, and interior decorators disliked Prairie buildings because their simplicity and heavy use of built-in furnishings left little for a decorator to do. Interior decorators and home decorating magazines pushed the craze for revival styles. *Ladies Home Journal*, which had published several of Wright's early and influential Prairie designs, now turned to Tudor revivals and English cottages.

In Wisconsin, some architects and contractors continued producing Prairie style buildings well into the 1920s and a few were even built in the 1930s. Wright himself claimed that his last Prairie house was Wingspread, built in 1937 in Racine for Herbert Johnson.

Major Prairie Architects in Wisconsin

Louis Sullivan

Sullivan was born in Boston on September 3, 1856, the second son of immigrant parents. He did well in school, and entered the Massachusetts Institute of Technology at the age of 16. After only a year there, he got a job with an architectural firm in Philadelphia, but stayed only a short time before moving on to Chicago, which was rebuilding from the disastrous 1871 fire.

Louis landed a job with an architectural firm, but left in 1874 to study in Europe for a year. He got another job on his return in 1875, and in 1879 changed jobs again, this time going to work for Dankmar Adler, an architect and engineer. By 1883, the firm had become Adler and Sullivan.

The two men created a revolution in American architecture with their designs for office buildings, theaters, department stores, and hotels. (They also designed a few residences, but their practice was devoted primarily to commercial buildings.) Sullivan was a leader in developing a uniquely American architectural style called the "Chicago School" by contemporaries.

Louis Sullivan, in partnership, and alone after 1895, produced nearly 240 buildings throughout his forty-year career. The peak of his popularity and influence lasted from the mid-1880s to the late 1890s. After the partnership with Adler dissolved in 1895, and his short, disastrous marriage failed, Sullivan became increasingly difficult to deal with. Beset by personal and financial troubles, a heavy user of alcohol and drugs, unwilling to compromise his architectural preferences when dealing with clients, his practice deteriorated, especially after 1910. The later years of his career are best known for his designs for small Prairie-style bank buildings, including one in Columbus, Wisconsin, which was his last important commission.

Sullivan, penniless and forgotten by the public, died of kidney and heart disease on April 14, 1924, in Chicago. Among his last visitors was Frank Lloyd Wright.

William Purcell, George Feick, Jr., and George Elmslie

Purcell was born in Oak Park in 1880, and while still a young man became interested in the work of Frank Lloyd Wright, who was a neighbor. Purcell was graduated from Oak Park High School in 1899, and received his degree in architecture from Cornell University in 1903.

13

Purcell worked for Louis Sullivan for a short time in 1903, long enough to become fast friends with George Elmslie, who was a longtime Sullivan employee. Sullivan didn't have enough work to keep Purcell on, so the young architect ventured to the west coast, where he worked in architectural firms in California and Washington before returning to Oak Park in 1906. He and his Cornell classmate George Feick took an extended trip to Europe, then opened the office of Purcell and Feick in Minneapolis in late 1906. Feick (1881-1945) was an engineer. He stayed with the partnership until 1913, when he withdrew to go into the contracting business in his hometown of Sandusky, Ohio.

In late 1909, George Elmslie left Louis Sullivan and joined his old friend Purcell in Minneapolis. Elmslie was born in Scotland in 1871, where he received his only formal education. In 1884 his family came to Chicago, and by the late 1880s Elmslie had embarked on a career in architecture, working in the office of J. L. Silsbee with Frank Lloyd Wright and George Maher, then moving on to join Wright in the office of Louis Sullivan. In twenty years there, Elmslie became Sullivan's top assistant, and was largely responsible for many of Sullivan's designs in the early 1900s.

Purcell and Elmslie were in partnership until 1922, during which time they were leading proponents of Prairie architecture (though like other firms of the time they also designed in other architectural styles). They constantly preached the gospel of this "organic" architecture: "Form and Function, use and shape, may never be separated; they are one, all inclusive, without exception," they wrote in 1913.

Purcell and Elmslie designed hundreds of Prairie-style homes, banks, churches, and municipal buildings. The firm was known for its creative interior spaces, its open floor plans, and its pioneering use of large amounts of glass in banks of windows and in folding or sliding glass doors. At their peak, Purcell and Elmslie were better known and more highly regarded among architects than Wright (though they took many of their ideas from him).

Purcell and Elmslie were, like Wright, able to design a total building—including furniture, light fixtures, leaded glass and other decorative elements. They even designed check blanks for their banks.

After the partnership was dissolved, Elmslie continued practicing until the late 1930s. He died in 1952. Purcell, who by 1922 was in ill health, moved to the west coast and did little architectural work after leaving the firm. He died in 1965.

George Maher

Maher was born in West Virginia on Christmas Day, 1864. He attended school only until he was thirteen. By then he and his family lived in Chicago, and he began an apprenticeship with an architectural firm there. He soon moved to the large and busy office of Joseph Lyman Silsbee, where he remained for several years. Silsbee was a progressive architect, and his office must have been an exciting place for young Maher to work (especially since Frank Lloyd Wright and George Elmslie were there also).

The 23-year-old Maher left Silsbee in 1888 to begin his own architectural practice. By 1894 he was well established, having designed a number of homes for the northern Chicago suburb of Edgewater. He married and built a home in the suburb of Kenilworth.

By 1897, with the design of the solid and simple Farson House in River Forest, Illinois, Maher found his own unique style. Some historians do not consider Maher to be a part of the Prairie School because his buildings have a different feel than those of Wright and others at the center of the movement. Maher's buildings are more solid and massive than those of other Prairie architects. However, he did use many principles espoused by Prairie architects in his designs, including wide overhanging eaves, emphasis on the horizontal, and the use of natural materials. Maher based his designs on his "rhythm-motif" theory. Simply stated, his idea was to take two or three elements —a plant or flower native to the area of the building site, and a design element such as an arch—and use them in decoration and construction throughout the house to create a feeling of unity.

Maher had a very successful and influential practice centered on Chicago and its suburbs, though his buildings are found throughout the Midwest, including the cities of Wausau and Madison in Wisconsin. Though his practice was mainly residential, the nearly 200 buildings he designed during the course of his career include libraries, offices, churches, banks, and two buildings for Northwestern University.

After World War I, Maher, like many other Prairie architects, reverted to more traditional styles. Maher, who had suffered from depression for many years, committed suicide in September, 1926.

Robert Spencer, Jr.

Though Spencer is a Wisconsin native, only two of his buildings are located here —one in Delavan (it cannot be seen by the public), and one in Wisconsin Dells. Robert Spencer, Jr. was born in Milwaukee on April 13, 1864. In 1886, he graduated from the

University of Wisconsin with a degree in mechanical engineering. He then pursued additional studies at the Massachusetts Institute of Technology, worked for an architectural firm in Boston, and traveled and studied in Europe.

He took a job with a Chicago firm in 1893, and began his own practice in 1895. Spencer and Frank Lloyd Wright were best friends for a time, members of a group of young progressive architects called "The Eighteen." They had adjoining offices in a downtown Chicago building.

Spencer, who was a prolific writer, published the first major article about Wright's work in the *Architectural Review* in June, 1900. It was the first of many articles Spencer published in both architectural journals and popular home decorating magazines praising Wright's work and espousing the principles of the Prairie School.

Even so, before World War I, Spencer began shifting his attention away from Prairie-style buildings and returned to traditional historical revival styles. He practiced until 1928, when he took a teaching job in Oklahoma. In 1930 he moved to Florida, where he taught until 1934, when he took a job with the Federal government. He retired to Arizona in 1938, and died in Tucson in September, 1953.

Louis Claude and Edward Starck

Louis Claude was born in Baraboo, Wisconsin, in 1868. He attended school in Baraboo, then went to the University of Wisconsin in 1887. While at the university, he was employed by Allan Conover, for whom Frank Lloyd Wright had worked previously. Claude left the university and Conover in late 1889 to take a job with the firm of Adler and Sullivan in Chicago. After nearly two years with Sullivan, years when Wright and Elmslie were also there, Claude returned to Madison. After a brief stint teaching engineering at the university, he opened an architectural practice, and by 1896 was in partnership with Edward Starck.

Starck, the son of a contractor, was born in Milwaukee in 1868. He came to Madison with his family when he was ten. Little is known about his early life, except that he worked for architectural firms in Madison, Milwaukee, and Chicago before returning home to open an office.

Claude and Starck worked in a variety of architectural styles throughout their 32-year partnership. During that time, they designed hundreds of buildings in Madison and throughout the Midwest. In addition to homes, they designed schools, banks, government buildings, churches and commercial buildings. They also developed a thriving business designing libraries. They produced nearly forty for small towns throughout the Midwest, and they wrote extensively about proper library design. Louis Claude was probably the partner who was most interested in Prairie-style buildings, given his experience with Sullivan and his continuing friendship with Frank Lloyd Wright.

The partnership dissolved in 1928, apparently because of personal differences. Starck went into partnership with another architect and continued a successful practice for another decade. He died in October, 1947. Claude continued alone, and with few clients, until he retired in 1947. He died in August, 1951.

Percy Dwight Bentley

Bentley was one of the few architects of the Prairie School who never had direct contact with Wright, Sullivan or any of the other dozen or so major proponents of Prairie architecture. Bentley was born January 30, 1885, in La Crosse, Wisconsin, the son of a prominent local banker. He attended local public schools, then Ohio Wesleyan University and afterwards the Armour Institute (later the Illinois Institute of Technology) in Chicago, graduating from neither.

While in Chicago, he discovered the architecture of Wright, Sullivan, and other Prairie architects. He later said of Wright and Sullivan, "I became very much indoctrinated with both, so when I opened my office in La Crosse it plainly showed in most of my work, which was mostly residential." Bentley was in practice in La Crosse by 1910, and became an immediate success.

He hired Otto Merman, a local draftsman who had trained in Minneapolis, and the two transformed La Crosse residential architecture. Bentley's first designs were based on the work of others, especially Wright and Walter Burley Griffin, but his later Prairie houses began to display his own distinct approach to the style. (Like other Prairie architects, Bentley designed in other styles at his clients' request.)

Bentley gradually withdrew from La Crosse, and by 1920 was practicing in St. Paul, Minnesota. Merman and a number of La Crosse contractors kept the Prairie School alive in the city until well into the 1930s.

In 1936, Bentley, who by then had completely dropped Prairie-style buildings from his work, moved to Oregon and continued his architectural practice on the west coast. He retired in 1961, and died in Eugene, Oregon, in February, 1968.

Russell Barr Williamson

Williamson, who became a leading Milwaukee architect with a career lasting more than forty years, was born in Royal Center, Indiana, on May 2, 1893. He attended Kansas State Agricultural College with a major in architecture and engineering, graduating in 1914. Williamson spent the summer of 1913 studying drawing and sculpture

17

at the Art Institute of Chicago, where he became familiar with the work of Wright and Sullivan. Upon graduation, Williamson wrote to both, asking for a job. Wright hired him.

At this time, Wright had an office in downtown Chicago, though he also spent time working at Taliesin in Spring Green. Williamson probably worked in the Chicago office. Williamson's job included drafting, drawing renderings of buildings, and doing on-site construction supervision. He was the supervising architect on two Milwaukee projects—the Bogk house and the American System Built homes.

When Wright left for Japan at the end of 1916, Williamson finished several projects, then left the office. He worked for a short time in Missouri, then came to Milwaukee as a partner with developers Arthur Richards and Arthur Munkwitz. Williamson's job was to design manufactured homes for the company. In the early 1920s, he took a similar job with a different real estate company, but soon began his own firm.

Williamson had a unique approach to Prairie architecture. He worked from two basic floor plans, one of which was the plan for the Bogk house. He rearranged and modified the plans by using different roofs (flat or hipped), by moving interior spaces (e.g. putting the living room on different sides of the houses), and by enlarging or shrinking the rooms. He also mass-produced leaded glass windows, decorative trim, light fixtures, floor tiles, and sculptures. Clients could use one of Williamson's floor plans, add as many or as few of his decorative items as the client could afford, and produce a relatively inexpensive Prairie house. (Williamson used this technique for other housing styles also.)

As Williamson explained, "The musician, with an instrument having a limited number of notes, produces an endless number of compositions and variations. Similarly, when the architect is master of the situation, he can produce a great number of variations from the same set of forms." A good disciple of Wright, he added that the plan "must be an organic plan—that is, a plan developed from the logical working out of the various needs and requirements that must be satisfied; not the picking of an exterior or shape and making the interior conform to this shape."

Williamson's Milwaukee work included dozens of houses ranging from tiny bungalows to mansions, as well as apartments and duplexes, the Eagles Club and other large commissions. There are hundreds of Williamson's designs throughout the city and its northern and western suburbs.

Williamson designed Prairie style homes until the mid-1920s, though he worked in other styles as well. His career continued into the 1950s. He died in October, 1964.

Racine

3

Population 80,000. Location: Racine County in southeast Wisconsin south of Milwaukee on Lake Michigan. It is most easily reached via I-94. Take Wis. Hwy 20 exit into the city.

Courtesy S. C. Johnson Wax

Johnson Wax Administration Building and Research Tower
1525 Howe St.
Racine, WI 53403

Frank Lloyd Wright 1936, 1944

Free guided tours of the Administration Building are offered Tuesday through Friday at 9:45, 11:30, 1:00, and 2:45. No tours on Mondays, weekends or holidays. Tours begin at the Golden Rondelle Theater on 14th Street. Tour participants must be fourteen or older unless accompanied by an adult. For tour information, contact Johnson Wax Guest Relations, 414-631-2154.

Courtesy S. C. Johnson Wax

The Administration Building shortly after completion

Johnson Wax Administration Building 1936

In 1882 Samuel Curtis Johnson left an unsuccessful stationery store in Kenosha and moved to Racine to sell parquet flooring for the Racine Hardware Manufacturing Company. In 1886 he bought the flooring business from the hardware company. Soon after, he began selling a line of floor wax at the request of his customers, who often didn't know how to care for their flooring. By 1898 sales of wax, wood finishes and wood fillers exceeded flooring sales.

In 1906, Samuel brought his son Herbert Johnson, Sr., into the company as a partner, forming S. C. Johnson & Son. They expanded the product line to include brushes, varnishes, wood dyes, and other new products, and in 1917 discontinued the sale of flooring to concentrate on floor waxes, car waxes, and their growing line of home cleaning products.

The founding Johnson had a strong sense of civic duty, and from the first both father and son looked to ways to improve employee working conditions. They shortened the workday from ten to eight hours, initiated paid vacations and profit sharing, and always looked for the latest in factory efficiency.

Herbert Johnson, Jr., took over the company on the death of his father in 1928, and even during the Depression managed to keep the company profitable through the

Johnson Wax
Administration
Building lobby

21

Testing the column,
1937. Wright in
foreground.

Courtesy S. C. Johnson Wax

introduction of new products. As the company grew, Johnson began to look for someone to design an office building to house clerical and administrative employees.

A local architect drew up plans for a typical Beaux Arts building, which company officers rejected as uninspired. Wright, whose career had been moribund since the mid-1920s, was suggested by one of the company's public relations consultants, who was familiar with Wright's work. Few others in the company had even heard of Wright.

Wright showed the Johnson officials drawings he had made five years earlier for a proposed newspaper plant in Salem, Oregon. The main room of the newspaper plant was two stories high, supported by thin mushroom-shaped columns that tapered from top to bottom. Mezzanine offices overlooked the printing presses on the ground floor. Johnson officials were impressed. Here was a design that would make the kind of statement about originality and creativity that the company wanted.

Wright promised Johnson that he could design an office building that would cost $200,000 to build. It would house 200 workers, offices for company executives, a conference room, and a cafeteria. (By the time the building was finished in 1939, the total cost, including the Wright-designed furnishings, exceeded $800,000. Some of the cost overrun was simply Wright's lack of experience with 1930s building costs—he had so few commissions in the 1930s that he hadn't kept up.)

Wright also tried to get Johnson to move the new company headquarters out into the country, away from the south side industrial area near the factory, where land had already been purchased and cleared for construction. Johnson refused.

Unable to convince Johnson to change sites, Wright in 1936 did what he had done in 1904 with the famous Larkin building in Buffalo. He designed a structure that turned inward away from its surroundings, creating its own unique environment independent of its location. The uninspiring site didn't allow for Wright's trademark bring-the-outside-in approach to design. Instead, as he had done in 1904, he created a building with no windows in the traditional sense. In the case of Johnson Wax, he used tubes of clear Pyrex (a new material that until than had been used only for test tubes and similar industrial and chemical applications) instead of window glass. Bands of tubing let in light without giving a clear view of the outside.

Wright believed the workplace should be as beautiful as a church, and as spiritually uplifting. To this end, he wanted to install a pipe organ to give the workers suitable music to listen to while they worked. Johnson refused.

Wright's design, one of the landmark buildings of 20th-century architecture, is built of two layers of custom-made brick with cork insulation between. (Some of the brick was spirited away to use in the Jacobs House I, then being built in Madison on a very strict budget. See p. 121.)

The building is circled by bands of Pyrex tubing, enhancing its aerodynamic, rounded feel. Wright's insistence on tubing caused tremendous problems because it was not until some years after the Administration Building was completed that a silicon caulk that would prevent leaks between the 43 miles of tubes was finally developed. To solve the leak problem, the company eventually replaced some tubes with sheets of corrugated glass, and in other cases covered the tubes with a protective sheet of glass.

Pyrex tubing covers the second-story walkway

Jerry Minnich

The Great Workroom is one of the most famous interiors in the world. Supported by thin, tapering columns of concrete reinforced with a then-new kind of extra-strength steel mesh, the Pyrex tube skylights between the mushroom tops give a diffuse light to the three-story-high space. The column design was so radical that the Wisconsin Industrial Commission would not grant a building permit until a prototype column was tested, since Commission engineers weren't sure the columns would hold the twelve tons that each had to bear. In the test, the column held sixty tons.

24

The Great
Workroom

25

Surrounding the main floor of the workroom is a mezzanine, used for offices. Also in the main building were a cafeteria, a theater, executive offices and a conference room. A second-floor arched walkway of Pyrex tubing joins the workroom to an annex that originally housed the legal and marketing departments, and a squash court. Beneath the annex is a large carport.

The Johnson Wax Administration Building, along with Fallingwater in western Pennsylvania and the Jacobs House I in Madison, launched the nearly seventy-year-old Wright, whom many had considered a sort of architectural elder statesman, on the second phase of his remarkable career. From 1936, until his death in 1959, Wright was constantly in demand.

The company remains extremely proud of its building, and has made only those changes necessary to continue efficient use of the building. The concrete floor of the Great Workroom has been carpeted in Cherokee red to match the original concrete color. The in-floor radiant heating, which was another Wright innovation in 1936, is no longer in use, but the heating channels embedded in the floor are used now for computer cables. Wright's furniture, with the addition of new pieces, is still in use, with the famous exception of the three-legged secretarial chairs. Those proved impractical, as employees were constantly toppling over. A four-legged version was commissioned, and those are still in use.

Johnson Wax Research Tower 1944

By the early 1940s, the company needed additional laboratory space, as most product research and development was done in-house. Johnson sent Wright a copy of a memo outlining research needs and attached a letter that read, "We *insist* the building should be built on competitive bids...To be frank, Frank, we simply will not consider a financial and construction nightmare like the office building. It is a plain factory kind of job that should be built by an engineer or contractor...Yet because of its proximity to your masterpiece, it should have a relationship thereto and we feel it would be unfair to you and a mistake on our part if we didn't ask how you think you would want to fit into such a picture."

Wright wanted to fit into the picture by designing the laboratory. Johnson made a passing comment to Wright that the building perhaps should go up, since space at the site was limited.

The Research Tower

Courtesy S. C. Johnson Wax

Since Wright in 1929 had designed a new form of tall building that he hadn't yet been able to get built, he accepted Johnson's suggestion and produced a tower design using the structural system he had previously developed.

Construction was delayed until after the war, but finally began in November, 1947.

The 153-foot-tall Research Tower is a masterpiece of creative design. The heart of the tower is a 13-foot-diameter, hollow concrete core rising from a 54-foot-deep, solid concrete foundation also 13 feet in diameter. Wright called this a "tap root"

27

Courtesy S. C. Johnson Wax

Research Tower under construction

foundation, and he patterned it after pines and other trees with deep tap roots. The core contains the elevator and stairs, the ventilation system, and all the pipes, wires, and conduits for the laboratories.

Fifteen alternating square and circular floors are cantilevered from the central core, which supports the entire weight of the building. The walls, alternating bands of brick and seventeen miles of Pyrex tubing, provide no structural support. To assure that everyone can see how the tower is supported, Wright eliminated the ground floor, so it would be easy to see the concrete core rising from the earth.

Wright designed the laboratory space so that a square floor and the slightly smaller round one above, which was in effect an open mezzanine, were one unit.

28

Communication, he presumed, would be simple, since scientists could just lean over the railing to talk to those below.

Part of the Research Tower project was a single-story row of offices and carports enclosing a courtyard surrounding the tower. The offices connected with the Administration Building to create a unified complex of buildings, and the tower was connected directly to the Administration Building by a third-story covered walkway.

The Research Tower was completed in November, 1950. The final cost was nearly $4,000,000, considerably surpassing Johnson's original intention to build it for $750,000. Costs kept rising as designs changed, and in October, 1946, a final estimate of $2,000,000 was agreed to by Wright, who also agreed to limit his commission to $200,000, no matter how much the building eventually cost. (Much of the overrun was not due to Wright's optimistic estimate; it was the sudden and unexpected inflation immediately after World War II.)

The tower served the company well until the research department began to outgrow it. By the late 1970s, the entire department was moved to another building. The tower now stands empty. Current building codes greatly limit the uses to which the building can be put, and the company refuses to do remodeling that would destroy the architectural integrity of the building.

Getting there: Take Wis. Hwy 20 (Washington Avenue) east from I-94 to 14th Street. Enter the complex at the Golden Rondelle Theater on 14th Street.

The Thomas Hardy House

1319 South Main St.

Frank Lloyd Wright 1905

Private home. Not open to the public.

For Racine attorney Thomas Hardy, Wright designed a home that is considered a classic melding of a building and its site. The house cascades down a steeply sloping shoreline lot, affording spectacular views of Lake Michigan while providing almost total privacy on the street facade.

Wright designed the wood-and-stucco house on three levels. Yet, on this anything-but-horizontal site, he was able to create a classic Prairie house with the rows of windows, wood trim, and a hipped roof with wide eaves providing the horizontal elements.

Hardy house living room, about 1960

State Historical Society of Wisconsin

The home's lower level can be seen only from the lake side. This lower level contains the dining room, which opens out onto a terrace, as well as the kitchen, a bedroom, and the utility areas. The second and third levels, which are seen from the street, contain a dramatic two-story-high living room that faces Lake Michigan through a wall of tall windows. Two pairs of bedrooms, one on each side, come off the living

31

State Historical Society of Wisconsin

View of Hardy house from lake shore, about 1960

room at both street level and at the second-floor level, where they are connected by an open balcony. Visitors enter the living room through one of two entrances in the high wall that provides privacy in the garden.

The Hardy house was considered an anomaly in Racine. No one else wanted a Wright design until 1936, when the Johnson family commissioned the Johnson Wax Administration building, only a few blocks away. The house still stands out among the Greek revival, Victorian, and other traditional homes in the neighborhood, just as it did in 1905.

Getting there: Take 14th Street east from Johnson Wax to Main Street. Turn north on Main, and the Hardy house is on the right. Or, take Main Street south from downtown.

The Herbert Johnson Residence, "Wingspread"
33 East Four Mile Road

Frank Lloyd Wright 1937

Now a conference center. Visitors may enter Wingspread when it is not in use for a conference. Contact the Johnson Foundation, Box 547, Racine, WI 53401. Phone 414-639-3211, for information.

Herbert Johnson and his first wife divorced in 1934, when their son and daughter were small. In 1936 Johnson married again. His second wife had two children from her first marriage.

As the Johnson Wax Administration Building was then under construction, Herbert Johnson and his new wife decided to ask Wright to design a new home for their

33

Master bedroom wing ending in cantilevered sitting room

blended family on land Johnson owned at Wind Point, just north of Racine. Until then, the Johnsons had lived on the south side of town.

Wright, given an essentially unlimited budget, created a 14,000-square-foot home which he called Wingspread, because four wings pinwheel off the three-story-high elongated octagon that is the center of the house. Wingspread is the largest Wright-designed home ever built.

Wright called Wingspread the last of his Prairie houses. The home combines Prairie elements—horizontal lines echoing a relatively flat landscape, a central core around which different functions are set, low doorways opening into high-ceilinged living spaces—with his Usonian ideas, notably the concrete floors with the four-foot-square design grid incised into them, and the in-floor radiant heating (which never worked properly in such a large house and was abandoned.)

Wright designed Wingspread as a zoned house. Each of the four wings had a different function—children's bedrooms and playroom, master bedrooms and sitting rooms, kitchen and service area, and guest rooms and garages. Wright's Prairie houses often had this zoned approach, with kitchen and servants' quarters in one area, master bedroom in another, all meeting at a central living space. Wingspread is Wright's most extreme example of zoning.

Wingspread occupies the center of a thirty-acre parcel one-half mile west of Lake Michigan. The original entrance to the house was from Lighthouse Drive, which runs along the lakeshore. Wright designed the entry gate. He also designed a gatehouse and farm buildings for the property, which were not built.

The contractor for Wingspread was Ben Wiltscheck, who also built the Johnson Wax buildings. The house is built of bricks from the same Illinois brickyard that supplied bricks for the Johnson Wax buildings. Other building materials include cypress, cream-colored sandstone (like that used in the Johnson Wax buildings), stucco, and interior oak paneling and woodwork. The roof is of red tile.

Herbert Johnson suggested an initial floor plan, which had wings coming off a central living room. Wright took the simple design, made the central core an elongated octagon, creating in the process one of his most stunning living spaces, and spun four equal-length wings off the corners.

The four wings pinwheeling off the central core create outdoor quadrants that hold a swimming pool (adjoining the children's wing), a garden and large pergola covered with grape vines (between the guest and service wings), the driveway (adjoining the guest and garage wing), and terraces (between the master bedroom and children's wings).

The pyramidal central core, which Wright called a "wigwam," is lit by three tiered bands of clerestories as it rises thirty feet. The huge elliptical chimney tower holds five fireplaces—four around the base and one on the mezzanine. The central core held the front entry, the dining area, living room, and library, all separated by changing levels a few steps up or down, or by built-in furniture.

A spiral stairway leads from the mezzanine up to a glass-enclosed outdoor crow's nest, which provides spectacular views of the surrounding landscape and Lake Michigan in the distance.

Three of the four wings are long, low, one-story projections, but the master bedroom wing is two stories. The three single-story wings join the central core at ground level, but entry to the master suite is via the mezzanine. Having the bedrooms raised gave Wright a chance to end the wing with a daringly cantilevered sitting room, which many observers liken to the prow of a ship. The sitting room provides a lovely view of the artificial pond in the ravine below. The beautiful master-bedroom floors are of plywood cut in narrow strips and laid on edge to expose the layering, the same

35

technique Wright used for the floor of the drafting studio at Hillside School (see p. 165) a few years earlier. The lower floor of the master-bedroom wing originally contained storage areas.

Herbert Johnson's wife died in 1938, before Wingspread was finished. Wright convinced the grieving Johnson to complete the house, and in 1939 Johnson moved in. The house is the subject of many famous stories. The most commonly repeated (and apparently true) story involves the unique dining table and the leaky roof.

The house had a dining table that was designed to be slid into the kitchen between courses, so the servants could clear the table and put on the next course without leaving the kitchen. (It's not clear whether this was Johnson's idea or Wright's.) For the sliding table to work meant that the location of the table and surrounding chairs in the dining area was fixed. Johnson had a number of distinguished guests to dinner one evening, when a thunderstorm began. Soon the roof (or rather, the seals around the clerestories) began to leak, dripping water down on Johnson. He was so angry, and probably embarrassed in front of his guests, that he immediately called Wright on the phone and loudly complained about the leaks. "Well," Wright replied calmly, "why don't you move your chair?"

The seal around the clerestories was finally fixed, and the leaks are now just a humorous memory.

Herbert Johnson eventually married a woman who didn't like Wingspread, and didn't particularly get along with Wright. She had a conventional home built right next to Wingspread, where she spent considerable time. Nevertheless, the family lived in Wingspread until 1959, when Herbert Johnson turned it over to the Johnson Foundation for use as a conference center.

The four wings were altered to make the house usable for conferences. Garages were enclosed for office space, bedrooms refurnished for meeting rooms, the lower part of the master bedroom wing was remodeled for rest rooms and other group facilities, servants' quarters were turned into offices, and the playroom became a large meeting space. Through it all, the spectacular central core has been virtually unchanged. Many Wright-designed furnishings are still in place throughout the house.

The Wingspread grounds have been planted in shrubs, evergreens, and other trees as Wright envisioned. The Johnson Foundation acquired and placed many outdoor sculptures on the grounds. The house built by the third Mrs. Johnson is called "The House," and is also used for conference activities. Another building housing Foundation offices was recently added.

Living room with central fireplace and tiered roof

Getting there: Take Main Street north from downtown Racine to Four Mile Road, then go east.

Also of Interest

When you leave Wingspread, turn east on Four Mile Road and drive toward the lake. Turn south on Lighthouse Drive. You will pass the original Wingspread entrance. A short distance further are the circular buildings of the Prairie School, 4050 Lighthouse Drive, a private primary and secondary school designed by Taliesin Associated Architects. Visitors are welcome to stop and view the school.

37

State Historical Society of Wisconsin

Keland House from the southwest

The Willard Keland House
1425 Valley View Dr.

Frank Lloyd Wright 1954

Private home. Not open to the public.

Karen Johnson, the daughter of Herbert Johnson, met Wright when her father hired him to design the Johnson Wax Administration Building. She later spent some years living in Wingspread. She married Keland, who, as president of the Wisconsin River Development Corporation, worked with Wright and later with Taliesin Associated Architects.

The Kelands commissioned Wright to design a home for their ample lot in a then-developing area along the Root River northwest of downtown Racine. For the sloping lot, Wright designed a long, horizontal home that snuggles into the hillside above the river. The house, constructed of brick and horizontal board and batten under a low-pitched copper roof, is in three sections—a long bedroom wing, the two-story living area with guest rooms on the second floor, and a wing housing a playroom. The three sections come together at a central patio and garden.

Getting there: From Washington Avenue, go north on Wis. Hwy 31 to Spring Street. Turn east on Spring Street to Valley View Drive.

For General Travel Information

Contact the Racine County Convention & Visitors Bureau, 345 Main St., Racine, WI 53403. Phone 414-634-3293, or 800-C-RACINE

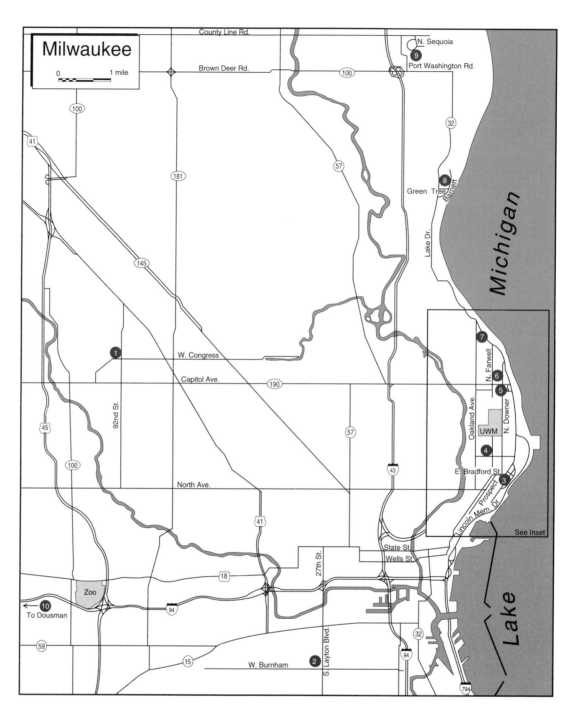

Milwaukee

0   1 mile

County Line Rd.

N. Sequoia

Brown Deer Rd.

⑨ Port Washington Rd.

Green Tree ⑧

Michigan

⑦

N. Farwell

W. Congress ①

Capitol Ave.

⑥

N. Downer

⑤

Oakland Ave.

UWM

92nd St.

④

E. Bradford St. ③

North Ave.

Prospect

Lincoln Mem. Dr

See Inset

State St.

Wells St.

27th St.

Zoo

⑩
To Dousman

S. Layton Blvd.

W. Burnham ②

Lake

① **Annunciation Greek Orthodox Church**
9400 W. Congress, Wauwatosa

② **American System Built Homes**
2714-2732 W. Burnham
1835 S. Layton Blvd.

③ **Fredrick Bogk House**
2420 N. Terrace Ave.

④ **T. Robinson Bours House**
2430 E. Newberry Blvd.

⑤ **Nathan Stein House**
Capitol & Harcourt, Shorewood

⑥ **Herman Newman House**
E. Jarvis & N. Farwell, Shorewood

⑦ **Russell Barr Williamson House**
4860 N. Oakland, Whitefish Bay

⑧ **Albert Adelman House**
7111 N. Barnett, Fox Point

⑨ **Joseph Mollica House**
1001 W. Jonathan, Bayside

⑩ **Maurice Greenberg House**
Hwy 67, Dousman

40

Milwaukee and Vicinity

4

Population 1,000,000. Location: Milwaukee County, on Lake Michigan in southeastern Wisconsin. Major highways serving the area include I-94, I-43, and U.S. Hwys 41 and 45.

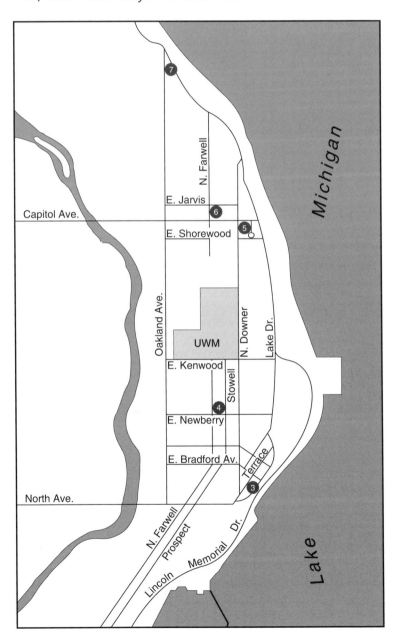

Frank Lloyd Wright had a long association with Milwaukee, beginning with his entry in an 1893 competition to design a library and museum for the city. (He lost.) He had a number of business and personal associates in the city, especially developer Arthur Richards and Wright's former assistant Russell Barr Williamson, who designed dozens of Prairie homes throughout Milwaukee County in the years after he left Wright's employ and became an independent architect.

Wright frequently turned to Milwaukee craftsmen to produce furnishings he had designed. Wright had an especially fruitful relationship with the Milwaukee company headed by George Niedecken, who had worked as an interior designer and mural painter for Wright in the Oak Park studio. Niedecken and his partner John Walbridge specialized in the design and execution of interior decorations, including furniture, art glass, light fixtures, and murals. Niedecken's company was responsible for executing Wright's interior designs for the Coonley and Robie houses in Chicago, as well as the interior of the Bogk house. Niedecken also worked for other architects, including Purcell and Elmslie, as well as carrying on his own independent interior design business. The Milwaukee Art Museum has a small collection of Prairie style furnishings, many of which are examples of Niedecken's work.

Wright also worked with other Milwaukee craftsmen, including the Matthews Brothers Furniture Company, the F.H. Bresler Company (furniture), and the Gillen Woodwork Company, which made the cabinets and other furnishings for Fallingwater, Wright's masterpiece in western Pennsylvania, and for Wingspread, the Johnson home in Racine.

Annunciation Greek Orthodox Church

9400 W. Congress
Wauwatosa, WI 53225

Frank Lloyd Wright 1956

Guided tours by appointment, 9-2:15, Monday-Friday. Groups only, fifteen person minimum. If you don't have fifteen people, call the church and they will add you to a scheduled group tour. Admission fee. Also, free tours are given continuously during the annual Greek Festival in early July. For information, contact the church; phone 414-461-9400.

As the Greek community in Milwaukee grew and became prosperous, the downtown church built in 1914 became too small, and too far removed from church members who increasingly lived in the suburbs to the north and west of Milwaukee. In 1952, church leaders appointed a building committee to search for a site for a new church, to begin fundraising, and to find an architect to design the church.

The committee wanted a church that would hold 800 for services, and would cost about $500,000. (As usual with a Wright building, this one cost more—$1,500,000

43

Interior from the balcony

by the time it was completed in 1961.)

The building committee began with a list of ten likely architects, none of whom was Wright. They had narrowed the list to four finalists in the fall of 1955 when Christ Seraphim, a new committee member, asked, "Have you interviewed Frank Lloyd Wright?"

One member of the committee thought Wright was dead. Others thought his services would be too expensive, or that he was too controversial. But Seraphim persisted that it would be unfitting not even to interview a Wisconsin architect who was by then known as one of the greatest America has produced. The committee agreed to postpone the vote and talk to Wright.

They went to Taliesin. Wright, and Olgivanna, who had been raised in the Greek Orthodox faith, charmed them. They voted 17-9 to ask Wright to design the church.

In 1956 Wright was at the peak of his career. In the last few years of his life he completed nearly seventy commissions, including major works such as the Guggenheim Museum in New York and the Marin County Civic Center in California. He was designing homes, theaters, medical clinics, university buildings, even a gas station (his only such design). He was also working increasingly with circular motifs.

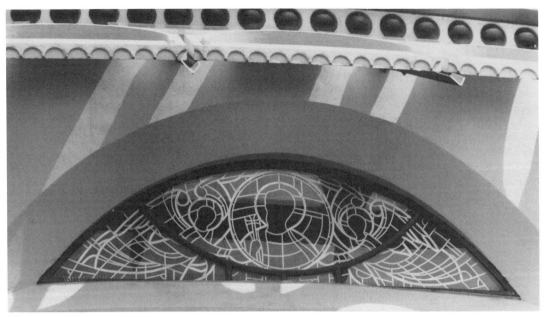

Detail of roofline and stained glass window

With Olgivanna's help, Wright learned the detailed Greek Orthodox traditions—what elements must be included in an Orthodox church. Then he produced a design melding Orthodox tradition with his own highly original style.

Wright's plan fuses two key elements of Orthodox churches, the Greek cross and the dome, into one unit. The church, a poured concrete structure, is a shallow dome resting on an equally shallow curving bowl, which, in turn, rests on a cradle shaped like a Greek cross. (To get a feel for the bowl, which is a mirror of the dome, go to the basement, where the ceiling is the gentle downward curve of the base of the bowl.) The Greek cross within a circle is a recurring decorative theme throughout the church; note the icon screen and other metal work.

The cross-shaped main floor holds 240 people in three arms of the cross, with the sanctuary in the fourth arm. A circular balcony above holds another 560 parishioners. Two spiral staircases with light trees in the center connect the balcony, main floor, and basement.

Arched stained-glass windows at the upper level, and 325 glass spheres just below the roofline, provide soft, constant illumination. (The stained-glass windows are not by Wright or Taliesin artists. They were completed in the mid-1970s by a studio from New Berlin, Wisconsin, and installed in 1978.)

45

The dome, a unique piece of engineering, was created by William Wesley Peters, Wright's chief assistant. It is 104 feet in diameter, and only 45 feet high from the center of the main floor. It is separate from the building—it rides on hundreds of thousands of ball bearings set in a steel track. Theoretically, it could be set spinning, though Peters designed it to allow for expansion and contraction during the change of Wisconsin seasons—not as a giant toy.

The color scheme throughout the church is gold and blue. The dome was originally covered with blue ceramic tile, but troubles with the roof required that the tiles be replaced with a blue vinyl membrane. Eugene Masselink, Wright's secretary and a gifted artist, painted the religious images in the icon screen.

In one of his last modifications to the design, Wright added a rectangular rear wing for classroom space. It joins the basement below the main level of the church, and opens out onto a sunken garden, so does not intrude on the lines of the church building proper.

Wright died in April, 1959, two months before construction began. Wesley Peters and other Taliesin architects supervised work on the church (and repairs to the dome when the tiles didn't work out). The building was finished in June, 1961.

American System Built Homes

2714-2732 W. Burnham St. and 1875 S. Layton Blvd.
Milwaukee

Frank Lloyd Wright 1911-1916

Private homes. Not open to the public.

Wright had a lifelong interest in low-cost housing. The American System Built Homes were his first opportunity to put that interest into practice.

Milwaukee developer Arthur Richards had worked with Wright on a 1911 hotel on Lake Geneva (now demolished). In November, 1911, Richards again engaged Wright to design a series of moderately priced apartments and single-family homes. (Manufactured housing was more common in pre-World War I days, with many small companies selling prefabricated homes. Customers could even order a home from a

47

American System Built bungalow

Sears catalog.)

Wright's interest in the project is indicated by the fact that he stuck with it through nearly six years. The American System Built file is the largest single file—more that 900 sheets of drawings, plans, and details—in the Taliesin archives.

The idea behind the System Built homes was simple. Since carpentry and finishing were such large parts of the expense of building a home, the System Built homes would eliminate the need for skilled carpentry by providing a kit of precut lumber. The System Built buildings were to be of stucco, plaster, and wood, and were modular designs based on a three-by-three-foot grid. Ideally, the modules could be fit together to build a wide variety of floor plans, ranging in price from about $2000 to more than $15,000.

Richards built the four identical duplexes and two versions of a bungalow in a southern Milwaukee suburb, in the middle of what was then a celery field. Construction of the six buildings was completed in 1916. In 1917 he and Arthur Munkwitz built two four-unit apartments (now demolished) using a different System Built plan on North 27th Street in Milwaukee. Three versions of the bungalow were built for clients in Illinois, and Wright used an American System Built bungalow plan as the basis for the Stephen Hunt house in Oskhosh (see p. 70).

American System Built bungalow

Unfortunately for Richards, the United States entered World War I in 1917, and the real estate market came to a standstill. He disbanded the American System Built company.

Richards later went into partnership with Russell Barr Williamson, Wright's former assistant and supervising architect during construction of the six Burnham Street homes. The two developed another manufactured housing system, which didn't sell well, either.

The six completed American System Built homes are examples of Wright's ability to get the most out of a modest space. The four duplexes have identical (though in one case, reversed) floor plans. Each apartment has two bedrooms, a bathroom, and an entry hall along the length of one side of the building. Along the other half of the apartment, separated from the bedrooms by a hallway, are the living room, a dining nook with built-in table and benches, the kitchen, and a sleeping porch.

The bungalows had two bedrooms, a kitchen and built-in dining nook, a living room, and a sun porch. Each had a slightly different floor plan depending on its size.

The smaller bungalow at 2714 Burnham St. is in nearly original condition, with virtually no changes since 1916. Although less than 1000 square feet, it feels spacious because of the light provided by rows of casement windows, the glass doors opening

49

onto the sun porch from the living room, and the higher ceiling and clerestories over the hallway. This central area has a raised roof that allowed Wright to create an open, airy space that doesn't feel like a tiny hallway. A large, purplish-red rough brick fireplace is the only separation between the living room and the hall.

The larger bungalow, on Layton Boulevard, was sheathed in stone veneer in 1956 (it was originally stucco and wood) and has been heavily remodeled on the interior, with the resulting loss of built-in furnishings, woodwork, and other design elements.

Three of the duplexes are still apartments and are relatively unchanged (with the exception of aluminum siding on one). The fourth has been converted into a single family home (the owners tried to be faithful to Wright's design and did as little as possible to alter the floor plans of each apartment). On all four duplexes, the sleeping porch was enclosed and winterized soon after construction, apparently in an attempt to attract buyers.

The Frederick Bogk House
2420 N. Terrace Ave.
Milwaukee

Frank Lloyd Wright 1916

Private home. Not open to the public.

A leading Milwaukee businessman, Bogk had interests in both a paint company and a real estate and fire insurance firm. He was also active in local politics, and served as a Milwaukee alderman from 1902 until 1920. Bogk undoubtedly came to Wright though his business and personal relationship with Arthur Richards, who had given several commissions to Wright, including design of the American System Built Homes (see p. 47).

51

Detail of 2nd floor facade

Wright's design for Bogk was a continuation of his work with solid, squarish structures of brick and concrete. The house, with its brick walls broken only by tall, narrow windows and its use of cast concrete ornament is a clear, but more refined, relative of Wright's Richland Center warehouse (see p. 186). Wright tried this type of design on several other residential projects of the period.

The Bogk house is of tan Roman brick on exterior and interior walls, with tall, inset windows. The main space of the house is a two-story square, with a small sun room extending from the first floor south wall, and a rear two story rectangular projection containing the kitchen and two bedrooms.

The home's main entrance is from the driveway on the north side. From a low entry hall, visitors go up four stairs into either the living room, to the right, or left and up two more stairs to the dining room. The main floor is open, with a large brick fireplace dividing the living and dining rooms. The living room is two steps lower than the dining room. Wright also designed a low brick divider that is both a flower box and a small pool (presumably for a water garden) between living and dining rooms. Upstairs, the home has five bedrooms.

Construction on the Bogk house, which eventually cost $15,000, began in August, 1916, and was finished a year later. Meanwhile, Wright sailed for Japan in December, 1916, leaving supervision of the remaining construction to his assistant Russell Barr Williamson.

Bogk lived in the house until his death in 1936, when it passed to his widow, Katherine. She and her sister lived there until Katherine's death in 1953, when it was sold outside the family. The current owners have carefully restored and maintained the home.

Also of Interest

Two blocks south, at 2220 N. Terrace Ave., is Villa Terrace Decorative Arts Museum. Built in 1923 as a residence for local industrialist Lloyd Smith, the house is a copy of a 16th-century Italian villa. It's a good example of the type of revival architecture Wright hated. Open 1-5 Wednesday-Sunday. Phone 414-271-3656.

The T. Robinson Bours House

2430 Newberry Blvd.
Milwaukee

Russell Barr Williamson 1921

Private home. Not open to the public.

By the time Dr. Robinson Bours asked Russell Barr Williamson to design his home, Williamson had left Wright's employ and had been working independently and with real estate developers for several years. During that time, Williamson had fully developed his ideas about the possibilities inherent in variations on one or two basic home designs. He believed that architects could produce virtually endless variations on a few basic floor plans, thus producing homes more cheaply. For virtually all his work, especially his work with real estate developers, he used variations on the Bogk house plan or on a basic bungalow floor plan.

Bours house from the southeast

For Dr. Bours, who had a long, rather narrow corner lot, Williamson produced an elongated version of his Bogk house design. The tan brick, concrete, and stucco house has many elements in common with the Bogk house: piers separating the windows on the front the house, the use of concrete ornament (in this case decorative concrete blocks on the second story front corners), the separation of living and dining areas by elevation (the living room is two steps lower), and the use of a brick room divider that contains a small pool of water.

Williamson, however, did not just copy the Bogk house. He lavished great attention on the Bours house and produced what is undoubtedly his masterpiece. The home, which cost $12,000, is lavishly appointed with leaded glass windows, built-in cabinets, and beautifully crafted woodwork.

The home is an excellent example of Prairie architecture. Its wide-eaved red tile roof, bands of decorative concrete, and rows of windows give the house a low, horizontal emphasis. Williamson also designed the garage and the wrought-iron fence

55

Bours house—detail of decorative concrete blocks

that faces Stowell Avenue.

The first-floor plan includes the living room with tall, narrow French doors opening onto a terrace. The main entrance is on the side, through the one-story projection that contains both the entry hall and the sun porch. A hall bisects the entire first floor, separating the living room in front from the dining room and kitchen, which occupy the rear half of the house. Upstairs are three bedrooms and a rear porch (now enclosed).

Williamson had several signature elements he used in designing virtually all his more expensive houses. Those include: stock leaded glass windows, of which he used at least three versions in the Bours house; the arched front door with clear panels of leaded glass; stock interior and exterior light fixtures (note those on the garage); decorative cast concrete ornamental bands and blocks on the exterior; and small plain rectangular tiles interspersed with small square decorated tiles for the living room floor.

Even though Williamson created a variation on one of his standard floor plans, he was able to produce a house that feels unique, exhibits a high degree of craftsmanship, and is extremely comfortable and interesting to be in.

The Nathan Stein House

3965 Harcourt Place
Shorewood

Russell Barr Williamson 1921

Private home. Not open to the public.

Williamson designed many variations on the Wright-designed Bogk house (see above). The Stein house is the one that from the outside looks most like a copy of Wright's design. It is simpler and smaller than the Bogk house, but Williamson manages to use virtually all the architectural and decorative elements found in the Wright design.

The house is a square with a dramatic entry hall and stairway projecting from the north side. Williamson used tall piers to separate the windows, as Wright did in the Bogk house, but instead of elaborate concrete ornamental panels as on the Bogk house,

57

Williamson used a thin row of one of his standard concrete trim designs.

The Stein house interior is less obviously a derivation of the Bogk house plan. The living room does take up the entire front of the house as it does in the Bogk house, and the living spaces are partially delineated by going two steps up or down, as in the Bogk house, but the floor plan in the Stein house is much simpler. The plan flows around a large central fireplace, which partially separates the living room from the dining room and the entry hall. A sun room and the kitchen occupy the rear of the house. Upstairs are four large bedrooms.

Williamson used a number of his stock items in the Stein house, including his small rectangular floor tiles, one of his leaded glass designs, and the light fixtures.

The Herman Newman House

2301 E. Jarvis St.
Shorewood

Russell Barr Williamson 1923

Private home. Not open to the public.

Herman Newman, who provided specialized insurance for contractors and builders in the Milwaukee area, asked Russell Barr Williamson to design a small but comfortable home for him and his wife. The resulting structure is one of the best examples of Williamson's use of his bungalow design, one of two standard home designs on which he based virtually all his residential work.

Williamson's standard design was for a single-story, two-bedroom home. Partway through construction, the Newmans decided they wanted a third bedroom, and Williamson added the partial second story to accommodate the extra room.

The exterior of the brick-and-stucco house is most notable for its dramatic projecting front entry, for the low, wide-eaved roof, and for the brick pilasters on the west side of the house, all of which give the home a strong Prairie feel.

The first floor carries out Williamson's standard bungalow floor plan. The main entrance is at one end of, and below, the living room. Four steps take the visitor to the level of the main rooms. A large L-shaped living-dining room surrounds the kitchen. To the rear are two bedrooms. All the rooms are centered around a small foyer that opens onto the kitchen, bathroom, living room, and downstairs bedrooms. The third bedroom occupies the second story.

The living and dining room windows, with rectangles of plain glass divided by leading, was a Williamson standard, used on a number of his lower-cost houses.

Mrs. Newman recalled that when she and her husband moved into the house, her mother-in-law was extremely upset that the young couple had built such a radical house. There was no proper delineation between the rooms, in the elder Mrs. Newman's view. She refused to speak to young Mrs. Newman for a time.

Also of Interest

One block north on Farwell Avenue are two homes designed by Williamson. The Agnes Keeley house, 4137 N. Farwell, is a lower-cost version of Williamson's Bogk house design. This house has only a living room, dining room, kitchen, and entry hall on the first floor, and three bedrooms on the second floor. A front terrace of concrete and brick has been removed. Four doors further north, at 4155-57 N. Farwell, is a Williamson-designed duplex. For these houses, he essentially used two of his bungalow floor plans, one on top of the other.

The Russell Barr Williamson House

4860 N. Oakland Ave.
Whitefish Bay

Russell Barr Williamson 1922

Private home. Not open to the public.

Within five years after leaving Frank Lloyd Wright's employ, Russell Barr Williamson was doing so well that he was able to build a substantial home for himself. Rather than use either of his standard Bogk-derived or bungalow designs, though, he chose another Wright building as his model.

In 1915 Henry Allen of Wichita, Kansas, commissioned Wright to design a home for him. At the time, Wright was heavily involved in preparing plans for the Imperial Hotel in Tokyo and getting ready to leave for Japan. It is not clear how much involvement Williamson had in the design and construction of the Allen house, but he clearly was

61

involved, perhaps to the point of doing some of the design work as well as supervising construction. (The house was built while Wright was in Japan.)

Whatever his level of involvement, Williamson obviously liked the Allen house, because he designed a very similar one for himself.

The tan brick-and-stucco house is L-shaped, with a long two-story wing that contains the dining room, kitchen, and utility areas on the first floor, and bedrooms on the second floor. The base of the L is the one-story living room wing. Extending from the corner of the L is the porte cochere, placed near the main entrance, which is at a corner of the living room.

In the Allen house, the L wrapped around a terrace and Japanese water garden in a brick-and-concrete pool. Williamson settled for a terrace and no pool.

Williamson did furnish his home with the materials—floor tiles, light fixtures, leaded glass windows, decorative concrete moldings—that he mass-produced for all his clients.

With its low-pitched roof and wide eaves, its emphasis on the horizontal in decorative trim and in the alignment of windows, the house is a fine example of Prairie architecture. It was perhaps Williamson's last Prairie design. After he received a large commission to design the Milwaukee Eagles Club in 1924, he shifted to popular styles such as Mediterranean revival.

State Historical Society of Wisconsin

The Albert Adelman House

7111 N. Barnett Lane
Fox Point

Frank Lloyd Wright 1948

Private home. Not open to the public.

Benjamin Adelman, Albert's father, was a longtime Wright client, for whom the architect had designed a Milwaukee home and a dry-cleaning plant (cleaning was the Adelman family business). Neither was built. Benjamin finally got a Wright home in 1951, for his retirement in Phoenix.

In 1946, Albert asked Wright to design a home for him. The first plans were for a house that would have been too large and too expensive. The second version, which was built, is a one-story, 170-foot-long home with five bedrooms on one end, a large living room in the center, and a kitchen and dining room at the other end. A covered 40-foot-long walkway connecting the kitchen area to the garage joins the house at a right angle.

63

State Historical Society of Wisconsin

Living room, about 1960

Adelman wanted a stone house, but to save money he substituted buff colored concrete blocks. The walls are shaped like an inverted pyramid—every second row of blocks is stepped out slightly from those below so the building seems to get wider from bottom to top. Rows of half-height windows in the bedroom wing, and full height windows and glass doors in the living room, open the home to the outdoors.

To soften the rather harsh feel of concrete blocks and concrete floor (with Wright's standard radiant heating system embedded in it), Wright designed the house with cypress window frames, woodwork, and ceilings. The home was designed to have no plastered or painted surfaces. Ceilings, with exposed beams, follow the line of the slightly pitched roof. Wright also designed built-in beds, desks, storage units, and other furnishings for the house.

The home is set at an angle on its long, narrow lot to provide the most privacy and to take best advantage of the wooded ravine at the rear of the lot.

The Joseph Mollica House

1001 W. Jonathan
Bayside

Frank Lloyd Wright 1956

Private home. Not open to the public.

The Mollica house is a reversed version of the first Erdman prefab (see p.128). Contractor Mollica built the largest version of the prefab, with four bedrooms, a full basement, and a garage. The house, in a quiet residential suburb, faces a wooded ravine.

65

Bill Martinelli

The Maurice Greenberg House
3902 Hwy 67
Dousman

Frank Lloyd Wright 1954

66

Private home. Not open to the public. Cannot be seen from a road or other public area.

Dr. Greenberg visited Hillside School and immediately resolved to have a Wright home on his wooded and rugged forty acres in rural Dousman. Wright's design was to have been built of native limestone, as was Taliesin itself on a similar hillside site, but the flat-roofed, single-story home that was eventually built is of brick, concrete, and wood.

The house is in three sections—a kitchen-workshop-laundry area, the high-ceilinged living room, and a bedroom wing, wrapping around the brow of a wooded hill. A balcony cantilevering over the hillside from the living room, and rows of windows in the other areas, provide lovely views of the surrounding countryside.

Getting there: Take the Dousman exit (Wis. Hwy 67) from I-94, go south several miles on Hwy 67.

For General Travel Information

Contact the Greater Milwaukee Convention & Visitors Bureau, 510 W. Kilbourn Ave., Milwaukee, WI 53203. Phone 414-273-3950, or 800-231-0903.

5

Two Rivers

Population 13,500. Location: Manitowoc County in east central Wisconsin, on Lake Michigan. Access is by I-43. Take the Wis. Hwy 310 exit and go east into Two Rivers. The city can also be reached on Wis. Hwy 42, which runs north-south along the lake shore.

State Historical Society of Wisconsin

The Schwartz House
3425 Adams St.

Frank Lloyd Wright 1939

Private home. Not open to the public.

A *Time* magazine article on Wright appeared in early 1938, and in September of that year Wright's "House for a Family of $5000-$6000 Income" appeared in *Life* magazine. Two Rivers manufacturer Bernard Schwartz was intrigued by Wright's designs and the philosophy expressed in the two articles. He visited Wright, and asked for a version of the *Life* house.

Schwartz bought a lot on the East Twin River on the western edge of Two Rivers.

Wright's revision of his design produced one of his most charming Usonian houses. The 3000-square-foot, T-shaped home, which cost $18,000, is beautifully crafted of red brick and horizontal cypress board and sunken batten on a concrete slab. The design grid is a 3'6" square.

Edgar Tafel, the Taliesin apprentice assigned to oversee construction, notes in his book *Apprentice to Genius*, that Wright's design lacked adequate structural supports. Tafel quietly added steel supports, never mentioning that fact to Wright. Tafel explains that he, Wes Peters and other experienced Taliesin architects regularly added steel and other supports to Wright's designs when needed, with discretion and without mention of the fact to Wright.

The Schwartz house is an excellent example of Wright's ability to protect privacy with a severe public facade, while still opening the home to the outdoors. The street side of the Schwartz house shows only the cantilevered carport projecting from a plain wood and brick two-story building. It's even difficult to see the entrance.

What you see from the street is the top of the T. It contains the entrance and master bedroom on the first floor, and bedrooms, one of which has a roof garden on the carport, on the second floor. Also in this part of the house is the square, two-story-high kitchen, topped by a skylight.

A balcony along the second-floor bedrooms looks down on the tail of the T, which is a spacious living area. Full length French doors on each side of the living room open to a terrace and yard on one side, and to a sunken terrace on the other. (The master bedroom also opens onto the sunken terrace as well as into the living area.) A massive brick core contains two fireplaces. One faces into the living room from a side wall. The second fireplace mass projects at a right angle from the first and acts as a divider to separate a small library area from the rest of the living room.

The house is in its second ownership and has been lovingly cared for. The original radiant heating system still works, and with the exception of a new roof and the addition of an air intake for the larger fireplace, very little has been done to remodel the home.

Getting there: From downtown Two Rivers, take Jackson Street (Wis. Hwy 42) to 22nd Street. Turn west on 22nd Street, then north on Adams Street.

For General Travel Information

Contact the Lakeshore Development Bureau, Box 903, Manitowoc, WI 54221-0903. Phone 414-684-3678.

6 Oshkosh

Population 53,000. Location: Winnebago County in east central Wisconsin, on Lake Winnebago. The city is served by U.S. Hwys 41 and 45, both of which run north-south.

The Stephen M.B. Hunt House
1165 Algoma Blvd.

Frank Lloyd Wright 1917

Private home. Not open to the public.

Stephen Hunt was one of Wright's earliest repeat clients. In 1907 Wright designed for Hunt a two-story home in La Grange, Illinois, that was closely modeled after

Wright's 1907 "Fireproof House for $5000" for the *Ladies Home Journal*.

Little is known about Hunt's life and career, but by 1917 he was vice president of McMillen Lumber in Oshkosh, and he was building another Wright home. Hunt was apparently not a wealthy man, because both of his Wright homes were relatively modest. The Oshkosh home was a variation on the prefabricated American System Built bungalows Wright designed for a developer in Milwaukee (see p. 47). The Hunt home, however, was custom built and had a number of extras, such as leaded glass windows, that were not included in the Milwaukee homes.

Hunt's Oshkosh home is a low, one-story, two-bedroom stucco and wood dwelling built on a standard city lot on a busy street in an area that was already developed. (In fact, the Hunt house garage predates the house. It was built for the neighboring house, but when the lot was subdivided further, the garage ended up on Hunt's side of the property line.)

Though modest, the house is carefully designed to make the most of the confined area. The lot was filled in with several feet of dirt, and the poured concrete foundation rises nearly two feet above the level of the ground. This places the house slightly above the level of the street and the neighboring house. This elevation, combined with the wide overhanging eaves and an extra deep setback on the lot, provide considerable privacy. Passersby can see only the tops of the interior walls and the ceiling, even though there are rows of windows in the living room and bedrooms. A landscape plan for the lot was completed by Wright's son Lloyd Wright.

Though small, the house has an open, airy feel provided by the many windows and the open floor plan of the living-dining area. A large red brick fireplace dominates the living room (there is some indication that the fireplace may originally have been faced with stucco). In warm weather, the living area could expand onto the enclosed porch.

The house has been through a succession of owners, and has been altered on a number of occasions. Interior dividers between the living and dining rooms were changed, the main entrance door from the porch was altered, the basement has been remodeled for living space, some built-in furniture has been removed, and the rear bedroom was enlarged.

The current exterior color scheme—light stucco and dark wood trim—is similar to that of the original.

Getting there: To get to Algoma Boulevard, take the Wis. Hwy 21 exit off Hwy 41. Turn right on High Street, then left on Vine Street, then left on Algoma.

Also of Interest

Oshkosh has a colorful history that includes the making and spending of fortunes in the lumber business. The Oshkosh Public Museum and the Paine Art Center are housed in the former mansions of lumber barons Edgar Sawyer and Nathan Paine. The two buildings are two blocks down Algoma Boulevard from the Hunt house.

For General Travel Information

Contact the Oshkosh Convention & Tourism Bureau, Box 3001, Oshkosh, WI 54903-3001. Phone 414-236-5250, or 800-876-5250.

Beaver Dam

7

Population 14,000. Location: Dodge County, in east central Wisconsin. Access is on U.S. Hwy 151 and Wis. Hwy 33. Beaver Dam is 40 miles northeast of Madison.

The Arnold Jackson House
7655 Indian Hills Trail

Frank Lloyd Wright 1956

Private home. Not open to the public.

The Jackson house is one of the Erdman prefab homes (see p. 128). Arnold Jackson, who was Wright's personal physician, was associated with the Jackson Clinic

in Madison. His wife originally approached Wright to design a small weekend cottage for the Jackson's land just south of Madison. Throughout the early 1950s, Wright sent designs and Mrs. Jackson rejected them because all were too expensive.

When the Erdman prefabs came onto the market, the Jacksons decided to buy one in the interest of having a relatively economical Wright home. By this time, 1957, they had decided on a year-round home for their hillside lot because the city of Madison was spreading out toward what had once been quiet farmland. Their version of the prefab had a full basement and a two-car garage, an option Wright at first didn't want to provide.

Dr. Jackson died in the mid-1960s, and Mrs. Jackson continued to live in the house until she died a few years later. The house was then rented for more than a decade. By the early 1980s, land in the area had become valuable for development. New owners of the home wanted it torn down, but in deference to the Wright name, they offered it for sale for $1 to anyone who would move it to another location.

A young Beaver Dam man named Christopher Fecht bought the house and moved it to a site outside Beaver Dam, intending to restore the home and live in it. Unfortunately, Fecht was in deep financial trouble by the time the house was finally moved. He committed suicide. The house sat empty for two years until new owners bought and restored it.

Getting there: From U.S. Hwy 151 in Beaver Dam, take Wis. Hwy 33 east to County Hwy A. Go north on Hwy A to Indian Hills Trail.

For General Travel Information

Contact the Beaver Dam Chamber of Commerce, 127 S. Spring St., Beaver Dam, WI 53916. Phone 414-887-8879.

8

Columbus

Population 4,200. Location: Columbia County in south central Wisconsin. Access on U.S. Hwy 151, Wis. Hwys 16, 73, and 89. Columbus is 25 miles northeast of Madison.

Farmers and Merchants Union Bank

159 W. James St.
Columbus, WI 53925

Louis Sullivan 1919

Open Monday-Thursday 9-3, Friday 9-5:30, Saturday 9-11. Phone 414-623-4000. Visitors welcome. Groups please phone ahead.

By 1919 Louis Sullivan's career was all but extinguished. The man who inspired Frank Lloyd Wright and dozens of other major architects, who created some of the most important buildings in American architectural history, had fallen on very hard times. Between 1915 and 1919, he received only five commissions. Two of those were for banks in rural communities—Sidney, Ohio, and Columbus, Wisconsin. The Columbus bank was to be Sullivan's last real commission; before he died in 1924 he did two remodelings and minor decorative work, but he did not have the opportunity to design any more buildings.

J. Russell Wheeler, president of the Farmers and Merchants Union Bank, originally wanted a typical Greek revival style bank. His wife, however, had seen pictures of some of Sullivan's other rural banks (which she first thought were by Wright), and wanted something more like those. Sullivan's preliminary sketches scared Wheeler "to death," but "Mrs. Wheeler smoothed my feathers and talked me into going ahead," Wheeler said later. Sullivan spent considerable time in Columbus supervising construction, and he became friends with the Wheelers.

The bank he designed was indeed unlike anything seen in Columbus up to that time. The two-story-high rectangle of reddish brown brick with a one-story rear extension is elaborately ornamented with terra cotta and stained glass designed by Sullivan.

A series of five receding arches over the front entrance frame a stained-glass window. Below, terra cotta ornament of intricate design frames a dark green-black marble lintel bearing the name of the bank and its architect. On the Dickason Street side are five arched stained-glass windows with abstract designs by Sullivan. Extensions of the terra cotta ornament carry the decorative theme around the bank exterior. Finally, an arched stained-glass window in the rear of the building surrounds a stairwell that projects from the building proper.

The bank interior is long and narrow, with teller cages along one side facing the five arched windows. Balconies at either end look down on the tellers and customers. The rear balcony was used as office space (it now houses an exhibit detailing the bank's history), but the front balcony is inaccessible to everyone except the janitor and was apparently built simply to balance the design. Though narrow, the two-story-high building has a marvelous sense of light, airiness, and space. (Note the ornate terra cotta drinking fountain designed by Sullivan, and the stained glass and brass table lamp he donated to the bank.)

Since completion, Sullivan's creation has been the object of loving care by successive generations of bank officers and employees. In 1960, when the bank needed more space, its officers were determined to build an addition in keeping with the character of Sullivan's masterpiece. The Madison architectural firm of Law, Law, Potter and Nystrom was retained to design an appropriate addition. The Indiana company that supplied the original bricks was still in business, and produced the bricks for the addition. The American Terra Cotta Company of Chicago had Sullivan's original designs in its vaults. After 32 tests, the company finally came up with a color to match the original terra cotta, which had been weathering for some 40 years. The bank found a rice paper of almost identical color and texture to match the paper used on the original interior walls (and which is still in place).

Even long-time bank employees can't tell where the addition joins the original structure. So perfect is the match of brick, terra cotta, and architectural style, it appears even the drive-up window could have been designed by Sullivan.

In 1980 the bank was expanded once again. The adjoining building was demolished to make way for a new structure that relates to the Sullivan building only in the color of the bricks (left over from the 1960 remodeling). The addition is unobtrusive and slightly set back, allowing Sullivan's building to remain at center stage.

Getting there: Take Business Hwy 151 into downtown Columbus. Turn west on James Street and go one block. The bank is at the corner of James and Dickason.

Columbus Public Library
112 S. Dickason Blvd.
Columbus, WI 53925

Claude and Starck 1911

Open Monday-Thursday 10:30-5:30 and 6:30-8:30, Friday 10:30-5:30, Saturday 9-12. Not open 6:30-8:30 on Tuesday, Wednesday, or Thursday in summer. Phone 414-623-5910.

The Columbus Library Association was organized in 1877 with the donation of 54 books and the use of two rooms over a storefront. By 1897, when the library was moved into City Hall, it had grown considerably and was supported by public subscription. By 1910 it was clear that the library needed more space, and the Columbus Women's Civic Club submitted an application for a $10,000 Carnegie Foundation grant for a new library building.

79

When the grant was approved, the city hired Claude and Starck, who were well known for their library designs, to produce plans for the new facility. The firm, which worked in both classical and more "modern" (later called Prairie School) styles, had designed libraries for Evansville (see p. 141), Delavan, Baraboo, Ladysmith, and a number of other communities in Wisconsin and surrounding states. The T-shaped stucco, brick and wood building dedicated on November 1, 1912, cost just under $10,000.

The Columbus library is unique among Claude and Starck designs in that it combines elements of Prairie style with English cottage decorative features. The building has a homey feel, with the recessed "front porch" and the flower boxes in the front windows—typical cottage touches. The building also has a vaguely Tudor feel, with exposed rafter ends and dark wood exterior trim.

Claude and Starck likely worked to give the building a residential feel because the library was located at the edge of downtown on a street that was commercial on one side (the Farmers and Merchants Union Bank is directly opposite) and residential on the other. The library, set back on the lot, blends well with the homes on the block.

Other elements of the building are typical of Claude and Starck's approach to Prairie architecture—the two front-facing gables, the grouping of windows high on the side and rear walls to allow maximum interior wall space for bookshelves, and the raised basement.

Originally, the main floor of the building included a fireplace, built-in bookshelves and periodical racks, benches, and a separate lecture room. The basement housed a community room and a kitchen and dining hall used by the Women's Club.

Recent alterations have removed an interior wall, expanded the side door into the main entrance, moved the half-hexagon librarian's desk to face the new entrance, and transformed the basement into a preschool. However, the alterations have left the basic character of the building intact, along with virtually all the original woodwork and built-ins.

Getting there: Take Business 151 to downtown, then go west on James Street one block to Dickason.

The Clarke Arnold House
954 Dix St.

Frank Lloyd Wright 1954

Private home. Not open to the public.

The history of the Arnold residence is one of those success stories seldom heard about Wright, perhaps because the stories of his artistic temperament and conflicts with clients have become such legends (and are certainly more fun to tell).

Attorney Clarke Arnold and his wife were friends of the Patrick Kinneys, for whom Wright designed a home in Lancaster in 1951 (see p. 192). One look, and the Arnolds wanted a Wright home, too. They bought an acre in what had been an alfalfa field on a hilltop on the edge of town and made an appointment with Wright. The local contractor was anxious to build a Wright design. Wright, or apprentice John Howe, who supervised construction, willingly made minor changes desired by the Arnolds as construction proceeded. Nearly forty years later, the Arnolds still live in and love their home. The fireplace works beautifully, and the roof doesn't leak.

The object of their affection is one of Wright's diamond module homes, a form he used in the Kinney House, the Smith House (see p. 85), and a number of other homes he designed in the late 1940s and early 1950s. In this design, all the angles are either 60 degrees or 120 degrees.

81

Living room and
bedroom wings

The low, one-story home of limestone, and redwood board and batten sits on a concrete pad, in which is embedded the home's radiant heating system (which still works perfectly).

The kitchen, dining and living room wing joins the bedroom wing at a 120-degree angle. After being in the house only a few years, the Arnolds, who by then had five children, asked for an addition to the home. Plans were completed but not executed before Wright died. The addition, with a bathroom and two other rooms, was completed by John Howe in 1959.

With the addition, the home is Y-shaped, with the flat-roofed new wing forming the tail of the Y, and the original bedroom wing and living-room wing wrapping around the terrace. The living-room wing and the new wing are visible from the street. As with most of Wright's residential designs, the view from the street is limited—stone walls and a row of clerestories. The other side of the home wraps around a terrace, with views of the shaded yard and of the surrounding countryside through the large windows and French doors in the living and dining area.

Getting there: Take Business Hwy 151 into Columbus. Fuller Street intersects the highway just south of downtown. Take Fuller Street to Dix Street, and turn north on Dix.

For General Travel Information

Contact the Columbus Chamber of Commerce, Box 294, Columbus, WI 53925. Phone 414-623-3699.

Jefferson

9

Population 6,800. Location: Jefferson County in southeast Wisconsin, midway between Madison and Milwaukee on U.S. Hwy 18. (Or take I-94, exit on Wis. Hwy 26, go south to Jefferson.)

Jefferson Public Library
(now called the Carnegie Building)
305 S. Main St.

Claude and Starck 1911

Now houses offices of the Chamber of Commerce, local historical museum and art center, and an art gallery. Open 9-4 Monday-Friday, and 2-5 the last Sunday of every month. Phone 414-674-4511.

**Jefferson Library—
detail of entrance**

The Carnegie Foundation was responsible for the construction of literally thousands of public libraries in the early years of the 20th century. The citizens of Jefferson sent in a request, and received a $10,000 Carnegie grant to construct a library on land the Jefferson Promoters Club had donated to the city.

By 1911, Claude and Starck were well known as designers of small town libraries, having completed libraries for Baraboo, Darlington, Delavan, Evansville (see p. 141), Kaukauna, and a number of other communities in Wisconsin, Illinois, Michigan, and Minnesota. The firm was designing in both classical and more modern styles, and for Jefferson produced a modern design which we now consider to be pure Prairie style.

The library is a handsome, dark brown brick structure resting on a low concrete foundation. The low pitched roof has a broad overhang with decorative wood molding under the eaves. The entrance vestibule projects from the main building and brings visitors into an intermediate level between the basement and the main floor. This design is typical of Claude and Starck's small libraries. It provides light and ventilation to the basement, which was designed to be a community meeting area. The main floor is raised above the vestibule level.

Though the building is no longer used as a library, the original built-in bookcases along the walls, and rows of original leaded glass windows are still intact.

Alterations include the addition of acoustic ceiling tile, fluorescent lights, and vinyl flooring. The basement has been altered to provide space for offices and an art gallery.

Getting there: Main Street is Wis. Hwy 26. The library is on the south edge of downtown Jefferson.

The Richard Smith House
332 East Linden Dr.

Frank Lloyd Wright 1950

Private residence. Not open to the public.

In the late 1940s, there was a plan afoot to get Frank Lloyd Wright to design a new Jefferson County Courthouse. The project never materialized, but Ruth Smith, wife of local lawyer Richard Smith, became friends with Wright and invited him to design the Smiths' new home.

The resulting structure, on a large city lot fronting the golf course, is perhaps best known for the continuing complaints voiced by Mr. Smith for the entire 36 years he lived in the house. Among his complaints to the man he called Frank Lloyd Wrong: the bedrooms and bathrooms were too small, the house was cold all winter, it was too hot and humid in summer, and, of course, the roof leaked.

85

The house did end up costing nearly twice the original $35,000 estimate. To recoup some of the costs, over the years Smith sold virtually all the furniture Wright had designed for the house.

The Smith house is a single-story structure of southern Wisconsin limestone and cypress resting on a concrete pad. The wood walls are the three-layer, non-load bearing sandwich Wright became so fond of after the Jacobs House I (see p. 121). In the Smith house, the plywood core is faced on interior and exterior with cypress board and batten. Wright designed in-floor radiant heating for the house, which failed in the living area but still works in the bedroom wing.

The Smith house is one of Wright's diamond module designs, a form he also used in the Arnold house in Columbus (see p. 81), the Kinney house in Lancaster (see p. 192), and a number of other homes built in the late 1940s and early 1950s. In this design, all angles in the house are either 60 degrees or 120 degrees. Wright carried this theme through in the Smith house to the point of making drawers in the shape of parallelograms in built-in bedroom cabinets.

The floor plan is shaped roughly like a lower case h, with the long arm of the h, which is the bedroom wing, sticking out toward the street and ending in the carport. The bottom half of the h wraps the master bedroom, kitchen, dining and living area around a 200-year-old oak tree, which is the focus of the house. An equilateral triangle surrounds the tree on the original blueprints, and all grid lines for the design lead from this triangle.

Mr. Smith sold the home in 1987 to the current owners, leaving them with a major renovation project. Originally, the concrete slab on which the house rests was built out to surround the oak tree, leaving only a small triangular area of dirt around the trunk. The tree began to wither, and Smith removed the concrete slab, replacing it with flagstones. This changed the distribution of the building's weight, and the walls along the patio began to sink. Current owners jacked up the remaining slab and inserted structural supports to prevent the house from sinking further.

Getting there: Linden Drive crosses Main Street in downtown Jefferson. Go east on Linden for three blocks.

For General Travel Information

Contact the Jefferson Chamber of Commerce, 305 S. Main St., Jefferson, WI 53549. Phone 414-674-4511.

Delavan

10

Population 6,100. Location: Walworth County in southeast Wisconsin. On I-43 approximately 45 miles southwest of Milwaukee. Also served by Wis. Hwy 11 and Wis. Hwy 50.

The Lake Delavan Homes

Frank Lloyd Wright 1900-1905

Wallis-Goldsmith Summer House 1900
3409 South Shore Dr.

George Spencer House 1902
3209 South Shore Dr.

Charles Ross House 1902
3211 South Shore Dr.

Fred B. Jones Estate and Gatehouse 1903
3335 South Shore Dr.

A.P. Johnson House 1905
3459 South Shore Dr.

Private homes. Not open to the public. All the homes are along a two mile section of South Shore Drive. Take Wis. Hwy 50 east from downtown to South Shore Drive. With the exception of the Jones Gatehouse, the houses are not visible from a road or other public property. They are visible from the lake.

Frank Lloyd Wright's friend Henry Wallis, an Oak Park realtor, bought land on Lake Delavan, intending to subdivide and sell lots and to build a summer home for himself. As Wallis sold lots, he invariably recommended Wright's architectural services to the new owners.

At the time, just after the turn of the century, Wright was in his mid-thirties and had established a thriving architectural practice in Oak Park. He had built his studio in

1895, attracting to it a number of talented assistants. During the period from 1900 through 1905, major Wright designs included the Unity Temple in Oak Park, the Larkin Building and Darwin Martin House in Buffalo, and the Dana House in Springfield, Illinois. In addition, he designed a number of summer cottages for clients in Michigan and Ontario and many homes in the Oak Park area. His other Wisconsin work during the period included the second Hillside School (the one now standing as part of the Taliesin complex in Spring Green), the Robert Lamp residence in Madison, and the Thomas Hardy house in Racine.

Jerry Minnich

Wallis-Goodsmith Summer House 1900

Henry Wallis was Wright's first Delavan client, and for him Wright designed this two-story summer cottage with horizontal board and batten siding on the first floor and a stucco second story. Two parallel bands of narrow wood molding, one just below the eaves and one just above the board and batten siding, as well as the nearly flat roof and wide overhanging eaves, create the horizontal feel typical of a Prairie house.

The interior features an open floor plan, with the polygonal dining room adjoining the living room, which is dominated by a large Roman brick fireplace. In the

88

original plan, porches on the front and one side of the house offered views of the lake.

A Wright-designed boathouse was built, but later demolished.

While the house was under construction, the Wallis' only child died and Henry Wallis decided to sell the home. It was purchased by Dr. Peter Goodsmith and his twin brother, who had married twin sisters. They felt the house was too small, so they enclosed the side porch and changed the location of an interior stairway in order to enlarge the living room.

Subsequent owners continued to change the house. Remodelings included enclosing the front porch and adding rooms in the rear. The house also stood empty for a number of years, and sustained considerable water damage.

Current owners are restoring the home to a state more nearly like the original.

Jerry Minnich

George Spencer House 1902

This smallest of the Delavan houses is the subject of one of the many stories about Wright and his artistic temperament. Wright supposedly intended the home to be sheathed in horizontal board and batten siding. He is said to have disowned the house when he found that the second floor siding was being laid vertically rather than horizontally (it was horizontal on the first floor). This story is not true, since original plans for the home show vertical siding on the second floor.

The Spencers had a long and narrow lot with little lake frontage. Wright designed for them a house with its front porch pointing toward the lake like the prow of a boat, giving it a vaguely nautical feel.

The original floor plan had an open first floor with kitchen, dining, and living areas surrounding a brick fireplace. The second floor had three bedrooms. There was no indoor plumbing.

In 1981 the guest cottage burned, and rather than rebuild it, the owner added new bedrooms and bathrooms onto the rear of the home. Fortunately, the addition blends well with the original home.

Charles S. Ross House 1902

This summer home, which is next door to the Spencer house, originally had three small bedrooms upstairs, one bathroom, and a porch and two verandas fronting on the lake. The home had its own water tower, which was filled with lake water that was used for all household needs except drinking. The home also had a primitive form of air conditioning: Three hollow columns linked the cellar to the dining room, and on hot days doors in the columns were opened to encourage a flow of cool air from cellar to dining room.

Since the 1920s, the house has been through a succession of owners and remodelings. The front porch and verandas were enclosed to expand the living room and add a library and sun porch. The second floor was extended over the front porch and interior walls on the second floor were removed to enlarge bedrooms and add bathrooms. The maid's quarters and original kitchen were remodeled into a new kitchen and breakfast nook. In addition, the unfinished cellar was remodeled into living space.

The remodeling has been faithful to Wright's designs, maintaining the roofline and horizontal exterior molding, relocating some of the original leaded-glass windows to the new sections of the house, and continuing the use of horizontal board and batten siding on the first floor and stucco on the second.

Fred B. Jones Estate, "Penwern," and Gatehouse 1903

Jones, a wealthy Chicago businessman and bachelor, wanted a summer estate where he could entertain friends. Wright produced Penwern ("Great House" in Gaelic),

Jones Gatehouse

a spacious party palace, complete with a card room in a tower connected to the main house by a covered walkway over the porte cochere.

The first floor of the wood-and-fieldstone main house featured two-story-high beamed ceilings, a billiard room, a massive living room and a banquet-size dining room. The row of windows placed high on the kitchen and pantry walls were probably designed to allow maximum work space, but local lore has it that they were high so servants couldn't look out at the goings-on and spread gossip.

The estate also included a water tower to hold lake water for domestic use, a boathouse (destroyed by fire in the early 1980s), stables (now used as a garage), and the gatehouse, which is now a separate residence.

In addition to the card tower (where no women were allowed), distinct design features include Roman brick fireplaces in the main rooms, and a second-floor balcony that offers views down into the billiard and living rooms and through the living room windows out to the lake. The arch appears throughout the house as a unifying theme —above the fireplaces, over the porte cochere, and supporting the roof of the front porch.

Jones owned the home until the late 1920s. The second owners lived there for fifty years, and the home is now in its third ownership. Though several rooms have been added in the rear, much of the original house is essentially as Wright designed it.

Minimal changes have been made to modernize and winterize the home, to make it suitable for year-round living.

The Jones Gatehouse, a wood and native stone cottage that was home to the Jones caretaker, has been extensively remodeled, first for winter use by the second owners of the Jones house, and now as a separate residence. Original features still intact include Roman brick fireplaces in two upstairs bedrooms and in the living room, as well as woodwork and window designs that echo the Jones house. Subsequent owners built a rear addition to the living area that incorporates a former back porch and storage room. Despite the changes, the facade of the house appears much as it did originally.

The tower connected to the gatehouse was used for water and equipment storage for two greenhouses that have since been removed.

A. P. Johnson House 1905

This house is the subject of a story that has Wright riding up the driveway on horseback and finding the home-in-progress painted white, rather than the dark color he had specified. At that sight, Wright allegedly turned around and rode away, refusing to have anything further to do with the house. The story has never been verified.

In any event, the Johnson family must have been pleased with their lakeside home, because they lived in it for more than sixty years. Wright designed for them a classic Prairie home, with low hipped roof, wide eaves, horizontal wood siding, bands of windows, a large central fireplace, and an open floor plan.

The home fell into disrepair in the 1960s, going through a series of owners and renters. The current owners have done massive restoration and remodeling work, including basic structural repairs.

Originally, the Johnson house had a living room that ran the length of the house, opening to porches on each end. Upstairs were five small bedrooms. The current owners removed interior walls to create a master suite and two smaller bedrooms upstairs, enclosed one of the porches, and remodeled the maid's room into a sitting room.

The wood tongue and groove siding is now painted cream with dark trim. We don't know whether Wright would approve.

For General Travel Information

Contact the Delavan Chamber of Commerce, 52 E. Walworth Ave., Delavan, WI 53115. Phone 414-728-5095.

Madison and Vicinity

Population 350,000. Location: Dane County in south central Wisconsin. Access via I-90, and I-94, as well as other major highways including U.S. Hwys 12, 14, 18, 51 and 151.

Madison is home to a large collection of both Prairie-style buildings by several important architects, and Wright-designed buildings spanning his career.

Wright lived in Madison from 1878 until 1887. While here, the family lived in a house at the corner of Gorham and Livingston streets on the near east side. (The house has long since been demolished.) He attended grammar school and high school here, spending summers on the Lloyd Jones farms in Spring Green. He enrolled at the University of Wisconsin, in January, 1886, as a special student. From early 1885 until 1887, when he left Madison, Wright worked for Prof. Allan Conover, an engineer and architect who was involved in construction of a number of University buildings. In his autobiography, Wright writes appreciatively of what he learned from working for Conover. He particularly remembered working on the construction of Science Hall: "At that time Science Hall was being built by a Milwaukee architect out of Professor Conover's office, the professor being superintendent of buildings for the University. So the young sophomore got a little actual contact with this construction. [Note: Wright never actually got beyond freshman status. Throughout his autobiography he frequently refers to himself in the third person.] He was entrusted with the working out of some clips to join the apex of the trusses of the main tower roof. They wouldn't go together and the workmen, disgusted, left them hanging up there against the sky by the few bolts that would go in.

"It was dead of winter—only the iron beams of the floors were in place in the floor levels below. All was slippery with ice, but he went up there, climbing the lattice on the chords of the trusses to the very top, with nothing between him and the ground but that forest of open steel beams. Got the clips loose. Dropped them down." Science Hall looks traditional and quite 19th century, but it was one of the first buildings with a structural steel frame.

The presence of the University and other progressive influences led many Madison home buyers and local architects to look beyond traditional architectural styles. As a result, the work of Prairie School architects is well represented in Madison, with more than seventy buildings by Wright, Louis Sullivan, Purcell and Elmslie, George Maher, Claude and Starck, and local architects and contractors.

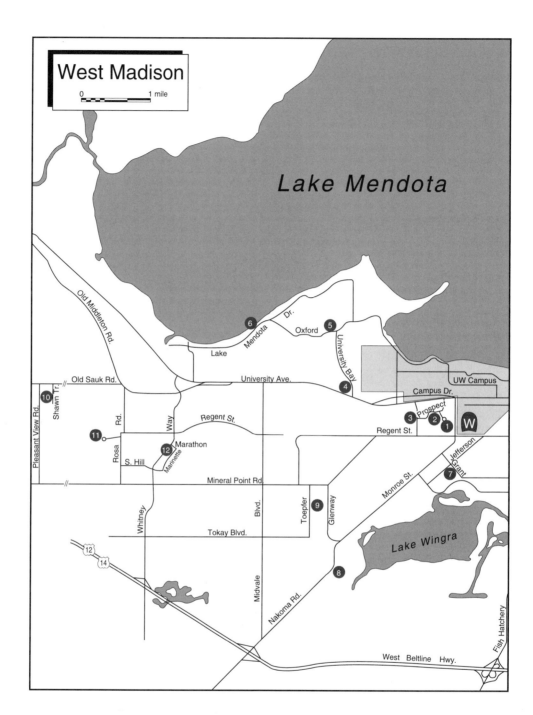

West Madison

0   1 mile

Lake Mendota

Old Middleton Rd.

Mendota Dr.

Oxford

Lake

University Bay

6

5

UW Campus

Old Sauk Rd.

University Ave.

4

Campus Dr.

Prospect

10

Shawn Tr.

Pleasant View Rd.

Rd.

Way

Regent St.

3 Prospect

2

1

W

Regent St.

11

Rosa

12 Marathon

Marinette

S. Hill

Mineral Point Rd.

Jefferson

Grant

7

Monroe St.

Whitney

Blvd.

Toepfer

9

Glenway

Lake Wingra

Tokay Blvd.

Midvale

12

14

Nakoma Rd.

8

Fish Hatchery

West   Beltline   Hwy.

1 Eugene Gilmore House
120 Ely Pl.

2 Edward Elliott House
137 N. Prospect Ave.

3 Harold Bradley House I
106 N. Prospect Ave.

4 Unitarian Meeting House
900 University Bay Dr.

5 Harold Bradley House II
2900 Oxford Rd.

6 John Pew House
3650 Lake Mendota Dr.

7 Cornelius Larson House
1006 Grant St.

8 Spring Trail Park
3700 blk. Nakoma Rd.

9 Herbert Jacobs House I
441 Toepfer St.

10 Herbert Jacobs House II
3995 Shawn Tr., Middleton

11 Eugene Van Tamelen House
5817 Anchorage Rd.

12 Walter Rudin House
110 Marinette Tr.

96

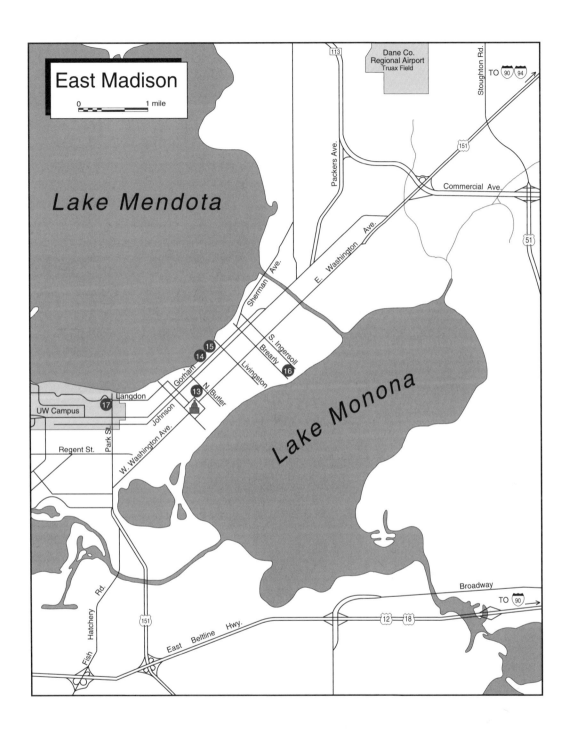

East Madison

0   1 mile

Lake Mendota

Lake Monona

Dane Co.
Regional Airport
Truax Field

113

Stoughton Rd.

TO 90 94

151

Commercial Ave.

51

Packers Ave.

E. Washington Ave.

Sherman Ave.

S. Ingersoll

Brearly

Livingston

15

14

16

13

Gorham

N. Butler

Langdon

UW Campus

17

Johnson

Park St.

Regent St.

W. Washington Ave.

Broadway

TO 90

12 18

151

Fish Hatchery Rd.

East Beltline Hwy.

13 **Robert Lamp House**
22 N. Butler St.

14 **William Collins House**
704 E. Gorham St.

15 **Lincoln School**
720 E. Gorham St.

16 **George Lougee House**
620 S. Ingersoll St.

17 **Science Hall**
550 N. Park St.

State Capitol

The Eugene Gilmore House

120 Ely Place
Madison

Frank Lloyd Wright 1908

Private home. Not open to the public.

In 1904, University of Wisconsin law professor Eugene Gilmore bought a large, fan-shaped lot at the highest point in the new subdivision called University Heights, which was hilly former farmland adjoining the western edge of the university campus. At the time, few houses had been built in the largely treeless subdivision.

He rejected the proposals of the first architect he retained, and was looking for someone a bit more creative when he came across Wright's essay "In the Cause of Architecture" in the March, 1908 edition of *Architectural Review*. Gilmore immediately contacted Wright, and by June had a set of plans for the concrete, wood, and plaster house that eventually cost about $10,000.

The year 1908 was the peak of Wright's creative success in his practice at his Oak Park studio. He and his staff of talented assistants were working on dozens of designs.

**Front entrance added
in the early 1930s**

In particular, he was immersed in construction of the Robie House in Chicago, and he was designing the Avery Coonley residence in River Forest, Illinois, another of his most creative (and famous) works. The Gilmore House is the only Madison example of Wright's work from this highly creative period.

At the time the house was built, Gilmore's lot offered some of the most spectacular views in Madison. From the top of the hill were visible Lakes Mendota, Monona, and Wingra, the Capitol, and the University campus. Only two homes, both down the hill, were built nearby. (Today, with other houses on adjoining lots, and mature trees, the views are somewhat obscured.)

Wright took advantage of the site by designing a cross-shaped home on a raised basement. Wright often used this approach to get the living quarters high above street level. It made for privacy and better views, especially in this case, where the lot was already in a commanding position. The basement contained storage and utility areas, the servant's room, and the home's main entrance, a low, narrow passage that led upstairs to the open, bright living room. Off the living room is a porch with a cantilevered roof. A high wall extends out from the porch, providing privacy for those in the garden. The first floor also held the dining room, library, and kitchen. The second floor contained four bedrooms, two of which, at opposite ends of the house, had triangular balconies.

99

The Gilmore house is classic Prairie School, with its low hipped roof, wide eaves, rows of leaded glass windows on both floors, the large central Roman brick fireplace in the living room, and the cantilevered porch roof.

Unfortunately, the cantilevering didn't hold up, because the contractor left out a steel support beam. The porch roof swayed ominously in the slightest breeze, so Wright built a bench in the middle of the porch supported between two pairs of sturdy floor-to-ceiling posts.

When the Gilmores left Madison in 1922, they sold the house to a medical fraternity, who in 1930 sold it to Howard Weiss, a researcher at what later became the U.S. Forest Products Laboratory.

When they bought it in 1930, the Weisses repaired and enlarged the house. They replaced the shingle roof with the present copper one, and they hired the Madison architectural firm of Law, Law and Potter to design two additions. The larger addition is in the rear, and contains garages, service and utility areas, and additional bedrooms.

The addition visible from the street is the new entrance. Instead of entering through the basement (though that entrance is still usable), visitors now climb an external staircase to a new entryway off the living room. The additions are faithful to the original in design and materials. However, the rear addition destroyed the symmetry of the house and obliterated the home's original "airplane" look. (Locals began calling it the "airplane house" almost immediately upon completion, apparently because the projecting roofs and balconies at different levels gave it a sort of biplane feel—at a time when the public was fascinated with the feats of Orville and Wilbur Wright.)

The home is in excellent condition, both inside and outside, with virtually all the original woodwork, many original light fixtures, nearly all the original leaded glass windows, and the built-in benches and sideboard intact. It is carefully cared for by a new generation of Weiss family owners.

The Edward C. Elliott House

137 N. Prospect Ave.
Madison

George Maher 1910

Private home. Not open to the public.

George Maher developed his own version of Prairie School architecture, one quite distinct from Wright's. When University of Wisconsin education professor E.C. Elliott commissioned Maher to design a house for his lot next door to Professor Gilmore's Wright-designed home, Elliott might not have known what he would get. Perhaps he expected a version of Gilmore's house, or one like the Sullivan-designed Bradley house two blocks away.

Instead of a strongly-horizontal design with rows of windows, cantilevered porches, and hidden entrances, Elliott's house is solid and straightforward. The two-story, hipped-roof structure is of a type Maher had developed a few years earlier, and which became enormously influential. Architects throughout the Midwest, including

101

Claude and Starck, borrowed Maher's basic design (and Maher himself used it many times).

The design is simple—basically a nearly-square rectangle with first- and second-floor sun porches projecting from the east end. The slightly tapering corners (actually just decorative extensions of the front and rear walls), are echoed in the gently tapering supports for the arched front entry. The slightly pitched roof with its wide eaves, and the five rows of battens encircling the second floor (all were originally a contrasting dark color, as was all the trim) give the house a horizontal emphasis, as does the centrally-placed planter box on the second floor.

Maher carried his "rhythm-motif" theory through in the Elliott house with a hollyhock floral design in decorative leaded glass panels adjoining the front door, in windows on the second floor above the entrance, and in a rear window on the stair landing. He carried the arch design into an arched-ceilinged entry hall, and he echoed the front entry in the living room fireplace, the outer edges of which taper gently from bottom to top, and are capped by an arch.

While Maher designed the house, it appears that Claude and Starck had a major role in actual construction. Elliott family records show payments to Maher, followed a year later by a smaller payment to Claude and Starck, apparently for their supervisory work.

Also of Interest

An example of how this particular Maher design influenced other architects is just two blocks down Prospect Avenue, diagonally across from the Bradley House. There you'll find the Sellery House, 2021 Van Hise Ave. (on the corner of Van Hise and Prospect). Designed in 1910 by a Chicago firm, it is an almost exact copy of a home Maher designed in 1907 for a suburban Chicago client.

The Harold Bradley House I

106 N. Prospect Ave.
Madison

Louis Sullivan 1909

Owned by Sigma Phi Fraternity. Free tours are available on a limited basis. For information, contact the fraternity at 608-233-5359.

University of Wisconsin Medical School professor Harold Bradley married Josephine Crane, daughter of Charles Crane, who had made a fortune in plumbing fixtures. Mr. Crane had commissioned Louis Sullivan to design two buildings for him, and he again turned to Sullivan when he wanted to build a home in Madison for his daughter and her husband.

The commission came in 1908, a time when Sullivan's practice was at a low point. For the structure that turned out to be his last residential commission, Sullivan initially created a home much larger than the Bradleys wanted. In 1909 he reconfigured the design into what was finally built—a roughly T-shaped, two-story home of brick,

103

Decorative brackets cover steel beams in the first Bradley house

wood, and shingles sheltered under a long, pitched roof with overhanging eaves.

The home, which cost $40,000, is best known for its marvelous cantilevered second story sleeping porches supported by steel beams covered with a wood facing.

Elaborate sawed wood ornamental designs cover the end of each beam.

Visitors enter on the north side, through the porte cochere and into a long gallery. Unlike the small, low, dark entry halls of some Prairie architects, this impressive beamed-ceiling gallery is long and flooded with light from a row of windows along one side. The gallery leads into the living room, off of which flow the dining room, the cozy octagonal library (which juts out from the house), and a large porch. The kitchen, which adjoins the dining room, completes the downstairs floor plan. Upstairs, there were bedrooms, playrooms, and the sleeping porches.

The commission called for Sullivan to design the furniture, rugs, draperies, light fixtures, leaded glass, and other decorative elements. George Elmslie, who was just on the verge of leaving Sullivan's employ after twenty years, was largely responsible for the interior (the extent of his contribution to the overall design of the house is a point of continuing discussion among historians).

The house was completed in 1910, after Elmslie had left Sullivan's office. However, Elmslie, and the firm of Claude and Starck, worked on the house in early 1910, providing some final drawings, and finishing the woodwork and kitchen. (Sullivan apparently had little to do with the house once he finished the design.)

Even though they had forced Sullivan to scale down his original plans, the Bradleys still found the house as built to be too large and too costly to maintain. In 1915 they moved into a new house in Shorewood Hills designed for them by Purcell and Elmslie (see p. 111).

The Bradleys sold Sullivan's house to the Sigma Phi fraternity, which has owned it since. Approximately twenty fraternity members live in the house. In 1972 a disastrous fire destroyed much of the second floor and attic of the home. Alumni donors helped raise the $762,000 needed to rebuild and restore the home to its original 1909 appearance, including replicas of the original leaded glass windows, many of which had been destroyed over the years.

Changes to the house include modernizing the kitchen, winterizing the sleeping porches, and enclosing the porch off the dining room.

Unitarian Meeting House

900 University Bay Dr.
Madison, WI 53705

Frank Lloyd Wright 1947

Guided tours offered Tuesday-Friday 1-4, Saturday 9-noon, from mid-May through September. Other times by appointment. Minimum donation $1. Group tours by appointment only. The building is also open regularly throughout the year for concerts and other public events. For information, contact the Meeting House at 608-233-9774.

Frank Lloyd Wright's father was one of the original members of Madison's First Unitarian Society, which was organized in 1879, and young Frank was apparently involved in some church activities. The Society's original church, completed in 1886, was located one block north of the Capitol Square at the corner of Dayton Street and Wisconsin Avenue.

By the mid-1940s, the congregation needed a larger church. Manchester's department store also needed a parking lot. So in 1944 the Society sold its building to Manchester's for $105,000.

Wright had been a member of the congregation since 1938, and was the immediate choice to design a new meeting house. (The choice was not unanimous, though. One member opposed to his selection called Wright "arrogant, artificial, brazen...a publicity seeker, an exhibitionist, egotist...unscrupulous, untrustworthy, erratic and capricious." She didn't like his architecture, either.)

Wright convinced the congregation to move the Meeting House to the suburbs, to a site where he could design a building that embraced its site, rather than turning inward away from the site as he had done with the design of the Unitarians' Unity Temple in Oak Park in 1904.

After some searching, in early 1947 the congregation purchased a four-acre plot on a hill in the Village of Shorewood Hills, three miles west of downtown Madison. At the time the area included a few homes, and the fields of an agricultural experiment station stretching down the hill toward Lake Mendota. (By the time the church was finished, the neighboring Veterans' Hospital had gone up, and development of the area was in full swing.)

Wright's first drawings, completed in early 1947, followed the instructions of pastor Kenneth Patton to produce a design with multi-purpose rooms, a church that would be used throughout the week. Patton required a kitchen, a nursery, and classrooms, and he also wanted the minister's residence to be attached to the church.

Wright initially estimated that his four-unit design (lobby-kitchen-office, auditorium and hearth room, classrooms, and minister's residence) would cost $60,000, but by the time he had finished the drawings, his estimate increased to $75,000. The building committee had trouble finding contractors to bid, and estimates that came in were more than quadruple Wright's guess. Finally, the congregation turned to Marshall Erdman, a new, young, and eager local builder. Erdman estimated that he could do the job for just over $100,000, not counting Wright's fee, furnishings and landscaping. Erdman bid low because he wanted work, and he wanted to work with Wright.

Construction began in August, 1949. To save money, members of the congregation spent fall, winter, and spring weekends hauling a thousand tons of limestone from a quarry thirty miles west of Madison. As costs mounted, Erdman's crew donated work, Wright gave two benefit lectures, and he finally sent Taliesin apprentices to work at the site. Wright also waived all fees beyond the $6000 already paid him by the

State Historical Society of Wisconsin

Unitarian Meeting House under construction

congregation. Nevertheless, by the time all the bills were in, the church cost nearly $214,000. Wright gave up more than $11,000 in fees (architect's fees are usually based on a percentage of total costs), and Erdman lost $30,000 on the project. The church eventually settled its outstanding debts to suppliers for 70% of the amounts owed. (Erdman didn't lose in the long run. His firm got business from those who figured that, since he was working with Wright, he must know what he was doing. One of his next projects was Doctors Park, a complex of medical buildings just south of the Meeting House.)

The building that put the congregation through physical and fiscal hell for nearly four years is considered by the American Institute of Architects to be one of Wright's most significant buildings. The limestone, oak, and glass structure wraps gracefully

Unitarian Meeting House from the southwest

around the hillside, two low, copper-roofed wings spreading outward from the soaring auditorium, with its peaked prow rising forty feet above the ground.

The church contains many elements Wright used in his Usonian houses. It is built on a four-foot diamond module, so all angles are either 60 or 120 degrees. The building sits on a concrete pad, into which is incised the diamond pattern, and embedded in which are the pipes for the radiant heating system.

The main entrance is beneath a sheltering overhang at the southeast corner of the building. Visitors walk into a low-ceilinged lobby area. Adjoining the lobby are restrooms, offices and the kitchen.

From the lobby, one enters the hearth room, on one wall of which is a large rough limestone fireplace. Only a change in ceiling height delineates the hearth room from the auditorium. For many years, a curtain, hand-woven by women of the congregation, separated the two rooms, but the curtain deteriorated and was removed. The domed ceiling in the center of the hearth room has a hexagonal wood band at its base, on which Wright had inscribed the names of notable Unitarians, including his uncle, Jenkin Lloyd Jones.

109

The walls and ceiling of the triangular auditorium rise gently from the rear to the spectacular glass and wood prow, which Wright viewed as a way to have the entire room become, in essence, the building's steeple. The prow was also supposed to serve as a bell tower, and a bell did hang for a time outside at its apex. Unfortunately, high winds caused the bell to sway wildly, and it was removed in the interests of safety.

(The auditorium prow as originally designed was to be of concrete blocks interspersed with stained glass, but was deemed too expensive and was changed to the current design before construction began. Perhaps a bell would have worked better with that more solid construction.)

At the front of the auditorium are the limestone and oak pulpit and the choir balcony. (Since the 1971 installation of the pipe organ, the choir sits with the congregation, on one side of the auditorium.) Two sound baffles project above the choir loft. Wright apparently added those at the last minute when he decided the acoustics were less than adequate. (They must work. Acoustics are now excellent.)

The movable pews, and all the furniture in the church, were made by Taliesin apprentices and members of the congregation.

The loggia, a long wing containing classrooms (originally there were eight, but removal of interior partitions has reduced that to four), connects the hearth room with what the congregation calls the "west living room." This open and sunny room was originally designed as the minister's living room, but Rev. Patton left before construction was complete and his replacement wanted a separate residence. Wright's original fourth unit, the bedroom wing for the minister, was not built, and the living room was converted to use as a nursery and a meeting and reception room.

The unfinished Meeting House was dedicated in February, 1951, but it was not until that fall that the building and its furnishings were actually completed.

Membership in the First Unitarian Society continued to grow, and in 1964 Taliesin Associated Architects designed the religious education wing using Wright's outline of the original minister's living quarters as a starting point for their design. In 1990, the congregation dedicated the Lower Meeting House, also designed by Taliesin Associated Architects, which is set into the hill behind and below the original Meeting House.

The Harold Bradley House II

2914 Oxford Rd.
Shorewood Hills

Purcell and Elmslie 1914-1915

Private home. Not open to the public.

Harold and Josephine Bradley found their Sullivan-designed home in University Heights to be too large and difficult to maintain. Sullivan had been difficult to work with, as he was apparently often under the influence of drugs or alcohol during their meetings. George Elmslie, who worked for Sullivan until late 1909, had conducted most of the meetings with the Bradleys, and they found him to be very talented and amiable. Accordingly, in 1912, when the couple wanted a summer home in Woods Hole, Massachusetts, they came to Purcell and Elmslie. And when they decided to build a new home in Madison, they again turned to their friend Elmslie.

Their second home, on a hill overlooking Lake Mendota, the University of Wisconsin campus, and the state Capitol, is a classic Prairie School house. The designers snuggled the house into the hill so that the basement opens out onto Oxford Road, making the home appear to be three stories high, while from the rear the home is clearly only two stories.

Roughly a square, the home appears to be long and narrow from the front, because the narrow projecting sun porches facing the lake hide the rear of the home.

The brick, stucco and wood structure places rows of second-story windows under a low, sheltering roof. Bands of wood trim enhance the horizontal design.

The house is beautifully preserved. A single story garage and service wing which was later added to the rear (not by Purcell and Elmslie) blends perfectly with the original structure.

The Pew House from the shore of Lake Mendota

The John Pew House

3650 Lake Mendota Dr.
Shorewood Hills

Frank Lloyd Wright 1939

Private home. Not open to the public.

Research chemist John Pew and his wife moved to Madison in 1930 when Pew took a job with the Forest Products Laboratory. They purchased a long, narrow lot with fifty feet of frontage on Lake Mendota in Shorewood Hills, a Madison suburb that was then mostly undeveloped.

Mrs. Pew wanted a Colonial-style house, so the couple contacted noted Madison architect William Kaeser. The plan he provided proved to be too expensive for the Pew's limited budget. Kaeser turned the Pews over to Herb Fritz, his draftsman. Fritz, who was just about to join the Taliesin Fellowship, convinced the Pews to try an entirely different style of house. They talked to Wright, and were soon converts to organic architecture.

113

The Pew house as seen from Lake Mendota Drive

Wright agreed to design a home for the Pews if they could widen their lot. Accordingly, they purchased an additional 25 feet of frontage, and Wright went to work.

The home he created for their sloping, uneven lot is considered by architectural historians to be one of his finest designs. The Pew house is a type of Usonian Wright designed for several other clients during this period. Called a raised Usonian by some historians, these houses are anchored to the ground at one end, but reach out over a slope or ravine and appear to end in mid-air. The Pew house spans a ravine. One side is firmly on the hill, the other is supported by a large limestone pier.

The home is designed in layers. The large living-dining-kitchen layer is wrapped on two sides by an open balcony. The second layer is created by a second floor open balcony. The third layer is the bedroom wing which rises to one side of the second floor balcony. Seen from the lake, the house appears to step up the slope, yet from the street only the square mass of the bedrooms (with a rectangular canopy over the windows at each corner) and the jutting carport can be seen. The house has only about 1300 square feet of living space, yet from the lake the balconies and the home's dramatic positioning as it appears to climb up the slope make it seem larger. From the street, it looks quite small.

The Pews couldn't find a contractor to build their rather unusual home, so Wesley Peters, Wright's chief assistant, became the general contractor. To save money (the Pews had only a $6700 budget, which had to include Wright's $600 fee), Peters scrounged the cypress, limestone and glass used in the house. (He also added steel support beams in places where Wright had underestimated the load.)

There are many stories about the Pew house construction. Peters remembered that the man charged with cutting trees on the lot to accommodate Wright's intended placement of the house cut all the wrong trees, leaving those marked for removal still standing. Wright calmly reworked the plan to take advantage of the remaining trees. One of the glories of the Pew house is its orientation on the lot. It does not face the water straight on, but is angled thirty degrees up the hill, providing views from two sides of the house rather than just from the front.

Another Pew house tale has it that Peters salvaged some building materials from a defunct tavern. The Pews awoke one crisp morning to find the ghostly words "Bar and Grill" traced in frost on the glass. They replaced that window pane.

The Pew house interior is as well known among architectural historians as is the exterior. The cypress walls are lapped like the sides of a wooden boat, so the walls are all off plumb from top to bottom. The hot water pipes for the radiant heating system are in a space under the wood floor. To allow free flow of heat, the floorboards are all spaced 1/8 inch apart. (The furnace is located in a small basement dug into the hillside.)

The Pews lived in their home until 1986, when they sold it to the current owners. The home is in excellent condition, having been well maintained and updated but never altered.

The A. Cornelius Larson House

1006 Grant St.
Madison

Attributed to Claude and Starck 1911

Private home. Not open to the public.

Banker and insurance company executive Cornelius Larson and his wife Della commissioned this beautiful Prairie house for their lot in the fast-growing suburb called Wingra Park. Cornelius was especially interested in the area, as his bank was involved in lending money to home buyers in the suburb.

The house, which is almost certainly by Claude and Starck (or an extremely talented imitator), is a two-story, dark red brick and tan stucco structure. The two front-facing gables, which project over the front terrace and entrance, echo Claude and Starck's designs for the Reedsburg and Columbus libraries (see pp. 154 and 79). Another Claude and Starck trademark is the pair of parallel string courses that wrap around the second floor at mid-window level. The bands of decorative trim under the wide eaves were also commonly used by Claude and Starck. The firm's trademark leaded glass design—narrow bands of colored glass along the outside edge of the window pane —is found throughout the house.

The home is essentially a rectangle with a porch projecting off the first floor on the Jefferson Street side. Note the second story windows above this porch. In a unique variation on bay windows, there are two pairs of windows, with each window in the pair projecting from the wall to meet at a 45-degree angle from the house, creating a tri-angular effect. Note also that the walkway to the front entrance runs diagonally across the front lawn from the corner of Grant and Jefferson to the front terrace.

After the Larsons moved out in 1940, the home went through a series of owners, and was eventually converted into apartments. Current owners are converting it back into a single-family residence.

Also of Interest

Across the street from the Larson House, at 1011 Grant St., is one of Claude and Starck's Tudor revival designs. This style must have been popular, because the firm designed at least four very similar versions for clients throughout Madison.

Farther west on Jefferson Street, in the 1800, 1900 and 2000 blocks, are examples of local variations on the Prairie idiom. Note especially the houses at 2015 and 2021 Jefferson Street. They were built in 1911 and 1909, respectively.

117

Did Frank Lloyd Wright design this? [Spring Trail stonework]

Spring Trail Park Stonework

Spring Grove Tavern Stonework
Both in the 3700 block of Nakoma Road
Madison

Attributed to Frank Lloyd Wright 1926

In University of Wisconsin Arboretum. Open daily. Parking adjacent.

In the mid-1920s, Madison Realty Company, developers of the new Nakoma subdivision on what was then the west edge of Madison, intended to develop a carefully planned and landscaped community, with boulevards, parks, a golf course, and other amenities. A small part of their plan involved creation of a park area surrounding two small flowing springs adjacent to Nakoma Road near the main entrance to the subdivision. They enlarged the small spring pond, set aside several acres for a park around the pond, and called it Spring Trail Park.

At the same time, the company hired Frank Lloyd Wright to design two large outdoor sculptures at the main entry to the subdivision. The statutes were to stand at the intersection of Nakoma Road, Manitou Way, Huron Hill, and Cherokee Drive (a spot about two hundred yards west of the newly-created Spring Trail Park). Wright's contract must have specified other duties, as the company's promotional literature stated, "Landscape architecture professor Franz Aust was retained by Madison Realty, as was Frank Lloyd Wright, to advise on preserving and increasing Nakoma's natural beauty."

Wright's design for the statues and reflecting pools proved to be too expensive, and in August, 1926, Wright and Madison Realty parted company, after Wright sent a letter criticizing their lack of vision, accusing them of acting like "a small man," and concluding, "let me abandon it and leave you free to deal with your landscape according to your light..."

Though no solid documentary evidence of Wright's work (such as plans, drawings, or letters) has come to light, local lore has it that Wright did produce one small piece of landscape work before he insulted the owners of Madison Realty Company and left their employ.

Popular history has it that Wright designed, and perhaps even helped build, the retaining wall along Nakoma Road, the stairs down to the springs, and decorative stone walls at the pond outlet, for Spring Trail Park. He also is credited with the design and construction of the wall directly across the street from the spring pond, in front of the old Spring Grove Tavern (now a private residence and local landmark; note the plaque on the wall).

At least one contemporary account, in the *Wisconsin Magazine of History*, mentions Wright as designer of the stonework, and Mrs. Leah Dickson, owner of the tavern at the time, recalled in 1971, "Frank Lloyd Wright and his stonemason built the stone wall around the place, Frank Lloyd was boss. I can still see him with his old brown leather britches, giving his ideas and council..."

Madison Realty promotional literature confirms that Philip Volk, a stonemason who worked extensively for Wright, did much of the stonework in the subdivision, and specifically credits Volk with building the stonework at Spring Trail Park.

Certainly, the stonework looks like a Wright design. The tan sandstone is laid in irregular layers in the same manner as the stone was laid at Taliesin (on which Volk also worked). A low wall along the road is broken near each end by two openings leading to stairs that wind down to the ever-flowing springs. Curving stone walls shelter and highlight the springs themselves as they flow from the base of the hill. At the pond

119

outlet, where the water flows toward nearby Lake Wingra, are two decorative stone walls that in size and shape echo the stonework surrounding the springs. The wall across the road in front of the Spring Grove Tavern is very similar to that of the spring pond.

There are two possible explanations for how Wright would have come to design the stonework. Either he did it as part of his work for the Madison Realty Company, or produced it for Mr. and Mrs. Dickson, who were his friends. Another possibility is that stonemason Philip Volk, who had worked extensively for Wright, simply did the work in a Wrightian style.

What do you think?

When you go to the spring pond to examine the stonework, be sure to take food for the flock of ducks who live there year-round.

Also of Interest

Three hundred yards west of the spring pond, at 3853 Nakoma Rd., is a fine Prairie home designed by Madison architect Alvan Small in about 1917. It was designed for Thomas Lloyd Jones, a cousin of Frank Lloyd Wright, and for many years owners and local residents attributed the house to Wright. Small, who worked for Louis Sullivan for a year, designed many Prairie houses in Madison.

The Herbert Jacobs House I

441 Toepfer St.
Madison

Frank Lloyd Wright 1936

Private home. Not open to the public.

Though Wright was considered an architect for the rich, throughout his career he was interested in finding ways to build reasonably priced homes for people of average means. So when Madison newspaper reporter Herbert Jacobs and his wife Katherine approached Wright in 1936 with a budget of $5000, Wright was immediately intrigued and agreed to design their home. (Due to Jacobs' decision to add a third bedroom to the plan, the house eventually cost $5500, including Wright's $450 fee.) So anxious was Wright to work on the project that he agreed in advance to a fixed-price $5500 contract—the only such agreement he ever made. The result of the Jacobs-Wright collaboration was the first of what Wright called his Usonian houses. (The term is derived from a number of literary and political references to the United States as Usona or Usonia.)

The first Jacobs house is considered one of Wright's most important works because it, along with the Johnson Wax Administration Building in Racine, and Fallingwater in Bear Run, Pennsylvania, signaled a new era of creativity and innovation in Wright's practice that lasted from the mid-1930s until his death in 1959.

Jacobs I was built over a period of six months in 1937, with Wright himself supervising much of the work of local contractor Bert Grove (who wanted the contract because he was eager to build a Wright design).

Wright hoped the 1300-square foot house would be a prototype for moderate-income housing of high aesthetic quality. In pursuing this goal, he incorporated a number of innovations. The house was designed on a two-by-four-foot grid to accommodate standard size sheets of plywood, which was cheap and was just coming into widespread use as a building material. This was one of Wright's first uses of a grid system, and he eventually used grids of all shapes and sizes in dozens of buildings designed throughout the remainder of his career.

The wood walls were screwed together in a three-layer sandwich, without the conventional studded framing, with plywood between identical interior and exterior pine and redwood horizontal board and batten siding. Wright believed this sandwich system could be mass-produced for use in prefab houses.

To save money, Wright designed the house with a flat roof, no attic, no foundation, a tiny basement just large enough for the furnace, and utilities grouped around a central core to permit short runs of pipe.

Heating was by steam (later changed to hot water) forced through steel pipes laid in the concrete slab on which the house sits. Wright was anxious to try this approach to heating, which he had discovered in the Orient, because he had designed it for the large and expensive Johnson Wax building, and he had never tested it. Fortunately, it worked (and still works in the Jacobs house), and was subsequently used in a number of Wright's buildings. Other money-saving innovations in the home include a carport and interior track lighting.

As a further savings the brick used for the fireplace, the utility core, and the supporting piers was culled from the Johnson Wax Administration Building, which was under construction at the same time.

The house was furnished with tables and chairs designed and built by Katherine Jacobs' cousin Harold Wescott, who had spent a summer at Taliesin and first suggested to the Jacobses that they approach Wright to design their home.

Placement of the house allows privacy and maximum use of the lot for gardening and other outdoor activities. The L-shaped house hugs a corner of the 120-by-126-foot double lot. The outer walls of the L that face Toepfer Street and the

Jacobs I from Toepfer Avenue

adjoining lot are broken only by a row of clerestories that run just under the roof line. This arrangement lets in light and ventilation while protecting the occupants' privacy.

The inside of the L wraps around a terrace and garden area. The walls of this side are almost entirely glass doors and large windows. Plans called for shrubs and trees on the remainder of the lot, but Jacobs did not carry out the landscaping plan.

One wing of the house contains three small bedrooms with low ceilings and a narrow hall. The other wing is the high-ceilinged, open living area, dominated by the massive brick fireplace and utility core. Included in the area is the dining nook, the small but open clerestoried kitchen, and the cozy bathroom.

The open-living-area floor plan, aiming for informality and efficient use of space, is clearly a forerunner of today's suburban ranch house.

Wright's manipulation of interior space with different ceiling heights, small and large rooms, and placement of windows to protect privacy on one side of the house while producing a feeling of openness to the outdoors on the other side, creates a home that is alive, stimulating, and interesting to be in.

The Jacobs family sold their first Wright home in 1942 to move to the country. They later built another Wright-designed home (an equally innovative earth berm, passive solar house) called Jacobs II by Wright scholars (see p. 125).

Jacobs I went through a series of owners and renters, including groups of students with assorted large animals, and had deteriorated badly by the time the present owner bought it in 1982. His extensive renovation included replacing the roof and part of the heating system, adding structural reinforcing at a few crucial points, cleaning and refinishing the outer walls, replacing rotted window and door frames, restoring the carport (which had been damaged when a neighbor's car rolled into it), painting the concrete floors, and adding a few practical improvements such as double glazing the large windows and improved insulation below the roof. The house appears today virtually as Wright designed it.

State Historical Society of Wisconsin

Jacobs II from the south, about 1960, before the current landscaping.

The Herbert Jacobs House II
3995 Shawn Tr.
Middleton

Frank Lloyd Wright 1944

Private home. Not open to the public.

In November, 1942, Herb and Katherine Jacobs moved from their Wright-designed Usonian to a 52-acre farm nine miles from downtown Madison in what is now the suburb of Middleton. They purchased the farm in order to get out into the country, and because they liked a potential building site on a hill near the farmhouse.

They intended to build another home as soon as possible, and began talking to Wright in early 1943. His first design was too large and expensive, but in early 1944 he produced a more modest design based on a semicircle. At this time, he was beginning work on the Guggenheim Museum, and was obviously interested in exploring the

125

The main entrance to Jacobs II is via this tunnel through the earth berm on the north side of the house.

design possibilities of circles. Just as the Jacobs' first home was the pioneering first Usonian, Jacobs II was a pioneer of passive solar design and was also the first of many buildings Wright designed based on circular forms.

His design for the Jacobs was a half circle protected on the north by an earth berm but open to the sun with large windows and glass doors facing a sunken garden on the south. Entry was from the north side, through a narrow tunnel in the berm, to a door in the south wall. The home had sweeping views of miles of farmland and open space.

The design is essentially one large limestone and glass room, 80 feet long and 17 feet wide, with only the kitchen downstairs and the bathroom upstairs given distinct separation through their placement in a masonry core. Otherwise, separation of functions downstairs was effected through placement of furniture. Moveable wood partitions separated the bedrooms on the second floor, which is a wide balcony hung by steel cables from the ceiling beams. A row of narrow windows just below the flat roof on the north side, and the open south side, provide natural light throughout virtually the entire day. The large south-facing windows provide passive solar heating in winter to augment the radiant heating in the concrete floor. To maintain the spare profile of the house, Wright eliminated a separate chimney, routing the fireplace flue so that the chimney was incorporated into the limestone kitchen stack that rises slightly above the roofline.

One of the unique features of the house is a small circular pool that is divided into halves. One half is indoors, and is used for a water garden. The other half is outdoors and is a small plunge pool in which Herb Jacobs and the Jacobs children cooled off on hot summer days. The halves are separated below the water line by concrete and above by the glass of the home's south wall.

Due to post-war shortages, construction didn't begin until late 1946. With the Jacobs acting as general contractors, and doing much of the work themselves, including hauling the limestone, the home was not finished until early in 1949.

In 1961, Herbert Jacobs left his reporting job and moved his family to California. Since then, the succession of owners have watched the suburbs eat away at the farmland in the area. The home is now at the edge of suburban residential and commercial development.

The Marshall Erdman Prefab Homes

The Eugene Van Tamelen House
5817 Anchorage Rd.
Madison

First prefab, Frank Lloyd Wright 1956

Private home. Not open to the public.

Also see Frank Iber House, Stevens Point (p. 223); Joseph Mollica House, Bayside (p. 65); Arnold Jackson House, Beaver Dam (p. 73).

The Walter Rudin House
110 Marinette Trail
Madison

Second prefab, Frank Lloyd Wright 1957

Private home. Not open to the public.

Throughout his career, Wright was interested in mass production of housing (see American System Built Homes, p. 47). In 1954, he discovered that Marshall Erdman, who had built the Unitarian Meeting House, was selling modest prefabricated homes. Wright offered to design better prefabs, ones that he believed could be marketed for $15,000, which was half again as much as Erdman was charging for his own version.

Wright didn't do much on the project until late 1955, but by spring of 1956 he had final plans for a Usonian-type home. His design was for a single story home with a pitched-roofed bedroom wing joining a flat-roofed living-dining-kitchen area centered on a large fireplace. A carport with one end of its roof resting on a detached storage shed completed the design. Eventually, Wright produced variations, including a fourth bedroom and options for a full or partial basement. The several versions ranged in size from 1860 to 2400 square feet.

To limit costs, Wright used standard Andersen windows and Pella doors, and designed the prefab to be built using standard sheets of plywood, Masonite, and drywall. The exterior was to be painted Masonite with horizontal redwood battens

Van Tamelen House

attached, though the house could also be built of stone or concrete block, or partially faced with stone.

The prefab package Erdman offered included all the major structural components, interior and exterior walls, floors, windows and doors, as well as cabinets and woodwork. In addition to a lot, the buyer had to provide the foundation, the plumbing fixtures, heating units, electric wiring, and drywall, plus the paint.

Before the buyer could purchase the house, he or she had to submit a topographic map and photos of the lot to Wright, who would then determine where the home should sit on the lot. Wright also intended to inspect each home after completion, and to apply his famous glazed red signature brick to the home if it had been completed as planned.

Erdman built a model prefab on Anchorage Ave. in fast-growing west Madison. Eugene Van Tamelen bought it in 1957. Erdman eventually sold seven of the first prefab model, including three others in Wisconsin. The other homes went to buyers in Illinois and New York.

The house didn't sell as well as Erdman had expected, partly because costs were often as high as for custom-built homes.

129

Rudin House

Wright's second prefab design was a two-story, flat-roofed, essentially square home of considerably more architectural interest than the first version. A band of clerestories under the roof gives the feeling that the roof is floating over the solid walls. The second prefab has a two-story-high living room lit by a wall of windows. A stairway leads to a balcony and the three second-story bedrooms. Under the balcony on the first floor are the dining area, kitchen, entry hall, utility room, and the master bedroom. A large concrete block fireplace separates the kitchen and living room. A carport attached to one corner of the house completes the design.

As with the first prefab, the second was built with Masonite siding with horizontal redwood battens and set on a concrete foundation. Again, Wright used standard materials such as Andersen windows to hold down costs.

A model home was completed in June, 1959. Erdman sold only two of the houses. The model went to University of Wisconsin professor Walter Rudin, and the other to a buyer in Minnesota. The model cost Erdman roughly $30,000 to build.

Though Wright had designed a third prefab before he died, Erdman never built or sold any of that design, and soon quit marketing the first two designs.

The Robert Lamp House

22 N. Butler St.
Madison

Frank Lloyd Wright 1903

Private home. Not open to the public.

Robie Lamp met Frank Lloyd Wright in 1878 or 1879, soon after the Wright family moved into Lamp's east side Madison neighborhood. They shared a common birthday, June 8, though Lamp was a year older, having been born in 1866. Wright remembered Lamp with considerable affection, and speaks at length in his autobiography about their relationship. They remained friends until Lamp's death in 1916.

Lamp, active in politics, was elected city treasurer in 1889, while he was still a student at the University of Wisconsin. He later got a job in the Wisconsin Secretary of

131

State's office, and then in the state land office. In 1896, he began an insurance and real estate business.

Though Wright had moved to Chicago and Oak Park, the two stayed in contact, and Lamp apparently helped Wright obtain two commissions for municipal boathouses on lakes Mendota and Monona. (The Mendota boathouse was built, but demolished in 1926. The Monona boathouse was never constructed.)

Wright also worked on three of Lamp's own projects. In the years from about 1892-1902, Lamp and a friend built and then rebuilt a weekend retreat on a tiny island off the northeast shore of Lake Mendota. While there is only circumstantial evidence that the three small 1892 structures were designed by Wright, there is considerable evidence that the 1902 rebuilding was a Wright project. The retreat, called Rocky Roost, burned in the mid-1930s.

In 1903 Wright designed a house for Lamp that was built at the rear of a large lot on North Butler Street. Immediately after, he designed a modest rental house for Lamp that was to have been built on one of two 33-foot-wide lots in front of Lamp's home. The rental house was never built, and Lamp sold the two lots in front of his house. The entrance to the Lamp house is between a brick home and a duplex now on those two lots.

The Madison *Democrat* of Sept. 6, 1903, describes Lamp's nearly finished house as a "new American type house" with "a number of features that are not found elsewhere in the city. Among these are the leaded casement windows throughout the house and the arrangement of brick so that the usual stone or wood window sills are avoided." The *Democrat* went on to say, "The cottage will be of white brick... Owing to the proximity of other buildings, Mr. Lamp will put on a flat roof and parapet wall, thus giving him a chance to swing a hammock and obtain a fine view of both Lake Mendota and Monona."

The Lamp house is stylistically related to Wright's other work of this period. The Lamp house, Unity Temple in Oak Park, and the Larkin Building in Buffalo, projects on the drawing boards at the same time, all are solid masses with hollow piers at the corners, though the Lamp house is obviously on a smaller scale than the other two.

The nearly-square Lamp house, with its side entrance (through a terrace and porch), central fireplace, L-shaped living-dining area, and four upstairs bedrooms, is considered by some scholars to be a forerunner of Wright's enormously influential 1907 design of "A Fireproof House for $5000," for the *Ladies Home Journal*.

Though the major features of the design were Wright's, some details, especially the decorative exterior brickwork, the diamond-shaped fireplace hearth, and the roof garden, indicate that Wright may have turned the project over to his assistant Walter

Burley Griffin, who eventually left the Oak Park studio and went on to become an important architect in his own right. (There are no documented Griffin-designed buildings in Wisconsin.)

In the early years of the 20th century, Wright's architectural practice was booming. Not only was he working on Unity Temple in Oak Park, and the Larkin Building and Darwin Martin house in Buffalo, he also had many smaller residential commissions. He had a number of talented assistants, and frequently turned work over to them to complete once he had roughed out a design.

Robert Lamp lived in the house first with his father and his aunt, and then with his new wife and her son. In 1913, Lamp enclosed the roof garden to make a playroom for his stepson. When Lamp died in 1916, the house passed to his relatives, but was eventually sold outside the family.

The exterior of the house has lost much of its original character. The third floor has been permanently enclosed, weatherized and rented as a separate apartment. An ugly set of enclosed exterior stairs was added to the rear and south side, and a fire escape was added to the rear.

However, you can get a feel for Wright's original design if you look at the east (North Butler Street) and north sides, and avert your eyes from the third floor addition.

The William Collins House

704 E. Gorham St.
Madison, WI 53703

Claude and Starck 1910

Operated as Collins House Bed and Breakfast by Barb and Mark Pratzel. Phone 608-255-4230

Lumber company executive Collins commissioned Claude and Starck to design a large home on his steep lot overlooking Lake Mendota. By 1910 the firm had developed its own distinct approach to Prairie architecture, of which the Collins house is a fine example.

The two-story, dark red brick home is built into the side of a hill, so that the full basement opens onto the lake side of the hill but is not visible from Gorham Street. The home is focused on the lake, with a porch the length of the house facing Lake Mendota, and a second story bedroom with doors opening onto a balcony and the lake view.

The pitched roof ends in wide sheltering eaves that are stucco on the underside, decorated with two narrow bands of wood trim. The dormers and gables also have decorative wood trim that echoes their triangular shape. A strong horizontal feature of the design is the trim which carries around the house at the level of the front second-floor window sills.

The design of the main entrance is one of Claude and Starck's trademarks—a door with an adjoining decorative wood and glass panel. (Some of their houses even have two decorative panels.) The leaded glass is also a typical Claude and Starck design—a narrow band of colored glass surrounding the clear center of the window pane.

The Collins house first-floor interior was originally dominated by three large rooms—the living room, library-entry hall, and dining room, each of which had beamed ceilings. In keeping with the house's orientation to the lake, the kitchen was on the street side of the house adjoining the dining room, which had the lake view. The three main rooms opened onto the porch, which is now enclosed and winterized. On the outer wall of the living room is a large gray-green ceramic tile fireplace surrounded by wide oak framing. Bedrooms occupied the second and third floors.

The Collins family lived in the house until 1935. It was then divided into apartments, and in the late 1950s was converted into city office space. In 1982, the offices were moved and the house stood vacant until 1985, when Mr. and Mrs. Pratzel began their meticulous restoration. The main floor of the home is now very similar to its original appearance. Much of the original oak woodwork and leaded glass is intact, as is the fireplace.

Lincoln School

728 E. Gorham St.
Madison

Claude and Starck 1915

Private apartments. Not open to the public.

Claude and Starck designed more public buildings than did most Prairie School architects. In addition to nearly twenty schools, they designed many libraries, city halls, fire stations, and other public facilities. Lincoln School is the finest existing example of their school designs.

The school, of tan brick trimmed in white stone and terra cotta, is built into a hill overlooking Lake Mendota. It is two stories high on the Gorham Street side, and three stories tall on the lake side.

Elaborate terra cotta ornament above the main entrances was designed by George Elmslie.

Claude and Starck's public buildings are simple, dignified, and efficient, in keeping the Prairie School dictum that form and function are intertwined. The Lincoln School is essentially a rectangle with the stairwells projecting from each end. The main entry was into a vestibule adjoining the stairwells.

The use of terra cotta and stone ornament is the most striking feature of the building. Three bands of ornament—at the base of the first-floor windows, and the continous bands at the top of the second-floor windows and at the roofline— provide a horizontal emphasis. Terra cotta ornament at the top of each of the pilasters that separate the windows, at the upper corners of the building, and over the two main doors make what would be an otherwise plain building a visual treat. The fine terra cotta work over the main doors was designed by George Elmslie for a bank in Minnesota. Apparently, he allowed his friend Louis Claude to use the design on the school.

Lincoln School closed in 1963, and the building reopened as the local art center. In 1980 the art center moved to a new home and in 1985 the building was sold to a private developer who converted it into apartments.

Also of Interest

Three blocks south on Blount Street is the City Market, a Prairie-style farmers' market designed in 1909 by local architect Richard Wright (no relation to Frank Lloyd Wright). Richard Wright had worked for Claude and Starck for a time, where he apparently became interested in Prairie design. The building was originally a large single room inside. After its use as a market ended shortly after World War I, it was used first as a dance hall, then as a city garage. In 1987, the city sold the building to a developer, who converted it into eighteen apartments. The exterior is largely intact.

One block east of Lincoln School at the northeast corner of Livingston and East Gorham Street (802 E. Gorham) is the site of Frank Lloyd Wright's boyhood home. That building was torn down in the mid-1890s, and in 1901 Claude and Starck designed a large home for the site for local businessman and politician Adolph Kayser. The Kayser home now houses professional offices.

Four blocks east of Lincoln School, East Gorham Street joins Brearly Street, which in turn intersects Sherman Avenue one block north. Along Sherman Avenue are a number of variations on the Prairie style. These homes are by Claude and Starck and by Alvan Small, a local architect who worked briefly for Louis Sullivan. Note especially 1004 Sherman Ave. (Claude and Starck, 1916), 1010 Sherman Ave. (Alvan Small, 1913), 1047 Sherman Ave. (Claude and Starck, 1916), 1106 Sherman Ave. (Claude and Starck, 1914), 1158 Sherman Ave., (Claude and Starck, 1915), and 1224 Sherman Ave. (Alvan Small, 1915).

The George Lougee House

620 S. Ingersoll St.
Madison

Claude and Starck 1907

Private home. Not open to the public.

     George Lougee operated a number of hotels and clubs, including the Park Hotel and the University Club in Madison, and the Palmer House Hotel in Chicago. He turned to Claude and Starck to design a large home for him in a prosperous east-side neighborhood.
     In the few years preceding, the firm had produced several designs modeled on the work of "progressive" architects such as George Maher. With the Lougee house, however, they plunged head-first into the Prairie idiom.

139

The house is a classic Prairie structure in the style of Frank Lloyd Wright. The two-story, L-shaped, stucco and wood home rests on a raised basement. The height of the house above the street, as well as a large low-walled front terrace extending from the southern section of the house, helps protect the occupants' privacy by making it difficult to see into the living room when standing on the sidewalk.

The architects created a horizontal effect with four bands of exterior molding at window-sill and window-head level on the first floor, and at window-sill level and at mid-window height on the second floor.

The first-floor interior was open and spacious, with a living room facing the terrace and other rooms flowing out from the living room and the central fireplace. Mr. Lougee apparently had a private library or office with a separate entrance at the rear of the house.

The building has been remodeled into eight apartments, and though the original floor plan was mostly obliterated, much of the original dark woodwork, including the beamed ceiling in the original living room, and many of the leaded glass windows, remain intact.

Also of Interest

The Lougee House faces Orton Park, one of Madison's most historic open spaces. Surrounding the park are a number of Claude and Starck homes that show the firm's ability to work in a variety of styles. The homes include a Queen Anne style at 1150 Spaight St. (1899) and its next-door neighbor at 1148 Spaight St. (1902), the firm's version of Tudor revival at 1125 Rutledge St. (1907), a Georgian revival mansion at 1115 Rutledge St. (1913), and a smaller home at 1047 Rutledge St. (1905).

For General Travel Information

Contact the Greater Madison Convention & Visitors Bureau, 615 E. Washington Ave., Madison, WI 53703. Phone 608-25-LAKES, or 800-373-6376.

Evansville

Population 3,000. Location: Rock County in south central Wisconsin twenty miles south of Madison on U.S. Hwy 14. From I-90, exit on U.S. Hwy 14 just north of Janesville and go north eighteen miles into Evansville.

Eager Free Public Library
39 W. Main St.
Evansville, WI 53536

Claude and Starck 1908

Open Monday and Wednesday 9:30-8, Tuesday, Thursday, Friday 9:30-6, Saturday 9:30-1. Phone 608-882-4230.

Detail of frieze

When he died in 1902, local merchant Almeron Eager bequeathed $10,000 to the City of Evansville to build a public library. His bequest had three stipulations: that the library be named after him, that it contain a life-size statue of him, and that the city operate the library. The city fathers happily accepted the donation, though finding a site and various other problems held up the project for several years.

The city retained Claude and Starck to design the building to house the 4300-volume library collection. At that time, the firm had designed a number of libraries for small Wisconsin communities, including Whitewater, Watertown, Baraboo and Stoughton.

Perhaps city officials didn't know what they were going to get, because Claude and Starck's previous libraries had all been of classical design. Increasingly, though, the firm was working in what it called an "original" style, the term "Prairie School" having not yet been coined. Evansville was the first Claude and Starck library of Prairie School design.

The building, dedicated in June, 1908, cost nearly $16,000, including landscaping and the cost of removing the building that originally stood on the lot. (Mr. Eager's widow, anxious that the project be completed as her husband envisioned, donated additional funds to complete the project.)

The library is a graceful structure, with a low, hipped, wide-eaved, red-tiled roof sheltering a red brick building on a raised concrete foundation. A terra-cotta frieze of abstract flower and leaf design provides a Sullivanesque accent. In fact, this style of library was called "Sullivanesque" by many people, since Sullivan was famous for his terra cotta designs. The frieze, originally bronze green, is now painted a cream color.

(Claude and Starck did not design the frieze. Such designs were commercially available to architects through firms such as the Architectural Decorating Company of Chicago.)

The building facade is pleasantly symmetrical, with a central entrance vestibule which deposits patrons at an intermediate level between the basement, with the community room and offices, and the main floor, where the library collection was housed. Large three-panel bay windows on either side of the entrance provide light for reading areas. A row of windows within the frieze also provide light while maintaining maximum interior wall space for bookshelves. Each window in the frieze (all are still intact) has a simple leaded glass design in pale green and lavender.

The original built-in bookshelves, a built-in high-backed bench near the entrance, a brick fireplace, and the librarian's office framed in with wood and glass partitions are still intact. The bronze statue of Almeron Eager, by Chicago sculptor Alice Cooper, presides over the patrons from its place of honor near the fireplace.

The library is in excellent condition. Alterations include changing the basement community room into a children's area, the addition of more bookshelves, and replacement of the original cork floor with tile. Also, the original hanging ceiling fixtures have been replaced by banks of fluorescent lights.

After the Evansville library, Claude and Starck produced libraries of similar design for Tomah (see p. 207), Merrill (see p. 235) and Barron (see p. 217), and they designed different, though equally fine Prairie School libraries for Jefferson (see p. 83), Reedsburg (see p. 154), Columbus (see p. 79) and Wisconsin Dells (see p. 149).

Getting there: Take Madison Street from U.S. Hwy 14 to downtown Evansville. Main Street crosses Madison Street in the center of downtown. Go one block west on Main to the library.

Also of Interest

Evansville has a lovely historic district that includes nearly 50 buildings representing a variety of architectural styles. A walking tour brochure is available at the library and at the Antiques Mall, 13 W. Main St., phone 608-882-4790.

For General Travel Information

Contact the Evansville Chamber of Commerce, Box 51, Evansville, WI 53536-0051. Phone 608-882-4230, or 608-882-4424.

143

13 Wisconsin Dells and Vicinity

Population 4,000. Location: Columbia and Sauk counties in south central Wisconsin. Access on I-90/94, on U.S. Hwy 12, and on Wis. Hwy 13. Wisconsin Dells is 50 miles north of Madison.

The Seth Peterson Cottage
Ferndell Road
Mirror Lake State Park
Town of Lake Delton

Frank Lloyd Wright 1958

Open year round as a guest cottage. For reservations and information, contact the Sand County Service Company, Box 409, Lake Delton, WI 53940. Phone 608-254-6551.

Public tours of the cottage are offered 2-5 p.m. the second Sunday of every month. An admission fee is charged. For tour information, phone 608-254-6051.

One of Frank Lloyd Wright's last residential designs was one of the smallest he ever produced. The Seth Peterson Cottage is an open-plan, one-bedroom home designed around a central fireplace. The cottage, based on a design Wright first developed in the 1930s, is built of locally quarried sandstone, pine, plywood, and glass. Original construction cost approximately $26,000.

The home contains only 880 square feet of living space, yet the large windows on the three exterior walls of the living area give it a feeling of spaciousness that belies its small size. The flagstone floor continues outside to form a patio bounded by low sandstone walls, extending the living area of the home outside and blending interior and exterior.

Seth Peterson was one of the first computer programmers for the State of Wisconsin. As a boy growing up in Black Earth, a village twenty miles from Spring Green, he became fascinated with Wright's architecture. He applied to join the Taliesin Fellowship, but was denied admission. He later requested a Wright-designed home.

Wright, who at the time was busy with such commissions as the Wauwatosa Greek Orthodox Church, the Marin County Civic Center, and the Guggenheim

Bill Martinelli

Museum, kept putting Peterson off. Eventually, Peterson sent him a $1500 retainer, which, Wright being Wright, was promptly spent. So Wright was forced to finally design the home.

Peterson intended to live in this home and commute to his Madison workplace. He also intended to marry. However, partway through construction he began having

145

financial problems. In addition, rumor has it that his bride-to-be jilted Peterson. Whatever the cause, the 24-year-old Peterson committed suicide before the house was completed.

A second owner finished the cottage and lived there until 1966, when the state bought it as part of Mirror Lake State Park. The cottage's remote location in the park made it impractical to use for park operations. Eventually, the park managers simply boarded up the deteriorating building.

In 1988 a group of local residents formed the Seth Peterson Cottage Conservancy and obtained a lease from the state to restore and operate the cottage as a vacation retreat. As such, it is the only Wright home anywhere that is available for public rental.

So badly deteriorated was the building that the $250,000 restoration required dismantling it down to the sandstone walls and fireplace core, which were the only sound portions of the building remaining, and then putting it back together.

The flagstone floor required particular care. The flagstones were photographed and mapped, each stone given a number. They were then removed, as was the concrete pad on which they were laid.

A new concrete pad, with pipes for the radiant heating system, was installed, and the flagstones were relaid. The new roof, electrical and plumbing systems, and windows were installed. Woodwork, including the stylized pine tree cutouts in the clerestories, were either restored or replaced.

The home is now virtually as Wright designed it, including double-glazed windows, the hot water radiant heating system, and a domed skylight over the kitchen, all shown in original plans but not included when the cottage was built. In addition, the cottage's Wright-designed furniture has been built and finally graces the space it was intended for.

Getting there: The cottage is on Ferndell Road in Mirror Lake State Park. The park is located off U.S. Hwy 12 south of Wisconsin Dells. Ferndell Road is the first intersection south of I-90/94 on Hwy 12. Follow the signs to Mirror Lake State Park. The Cottage is about a mile beyond the park office.

The Sherman House

930 River Road
Wisconsin Dells, WI 53965

Robert Spencer 1904

Operated May 1 - November 1 as Sherman House Bed & Breakfast by Mrs. Norma Marz.
Phone 608-253-2721.

J.M. Sherman, a wealthy Chicago attorney, commissioned Spencer to design this summer home overlooking the Wisconsin River. It is one of only two residences Spencer designed in Wisconsin (the other cannot be seen by the public).

The two story, fourteen-room, roughly L-shaped home, of buff-colored stucco and native red sandstone, features a porch with a spectacular view of the river. Spencer was a believer in porches, and he was especially proud of this one, featuring it in a 1905 article he wrote for *House Beautiful*.

The house has had only four owners since 1904, and is in excellent condition. Original wood molding bands virtually every room. The open living and dining area is

147

splendid, with back-to-back tan brick fireplaces forming two sides of a triangular divide between the two rooms. The point of the triangle directs the eye out through the wide doors opening onto the porch and to the river beyond. Above each fireplace mantel, Spencer placed a narrow horizontal oil painting of forest scenes. One painting is gone, the other remains.

The original carriage house, also of stucco, is still standing and is now used for storage.

Getting there: Take Wis. Hwy 13 into downtown Wisconsin Dells. Go north on River Road, which is the first stop light east of the Wisconsin River.

Kilbourn Public Library

429 Broadway
Wisconsin Dells, WI 53965

Claude and Starck 1912

Open Tuesday, Wednesday, Thursday 10-8; Friday, Saturday 10-5; closed Saturday in summer. Phone 608-254-2146.

In 1886 the leading women of the village of Kilbourn organized the Literary and Library Association. The society ran a lending library until 1897, when the village took over those duties, levying a library tax and providing a home for the library materials in the Village Council Room. In 1902, with the help of a local merchant, the Ladies Tuesday Club began a fundraising drive that produced enough money to buy a house and convert it into a library. By 1912 the library was bursting at the seams and the village

149

applied for a Carnegie Foundation grant for a new library building. They received $6000, to which the village added another $11,000.

With $17,000 in hand, they turned to Claude and Starck, who were well known for their library designs, having produced buildings for Baraboo, Delavan, Kaukauna, and a number of other small communities throughout Wisconsin and surrounding states.

By 1912 the firm had designed libraries in both classical and more "modern" (now called Prairie) style, including their "Sullivanesque" libraries in Evansville (see p. 141) and Merrill (see p. 235), and the firm's unique version of the Prairie style in Jefferson (see p. 83), Reedsburg (see p. 154), and Columbus (see p. 79).

For Kilbourn, Claude and Starck produced a unique design that combines the clean, horizontal lines of the Prairie School with decorative elements of the Arts and Crafts movement.

As with many of their designs, the sandstone, wood, and stucco building is a simple rectangle on a raised basement, with a projecting entry that deposits patrons at mid-level between the community meeting room in the basement and the library on the main floor. Large windows on each side of the entrance, and rows of high windows on the sides and rear, are typical of a Claude and Starck design. To the gable roof with generous eaves, typical of Claude and Starck's Prairie designs, they added Arts and Crafts elements in the triangular supporting brackets and the exposed beam ends. The vertical emphasis provided by the dark wood exterior trim is also a typical Arts and Crafts element.

The library interior is virtually unchanged, with intact wood molding, as well as the built-in bookshelves and periodical racks, the original half-hexagon librarian's desk with the large window directly behind, and the original card catalog. The basement has been remodeled to provide room for more bookshelves and for storage.

Getting there: Wis. Hwy 13 becomes Broadway in downtown Wisconsin Dells.

For General Travel Information

Contact the Wisconsin Dells Visitors & Convention Bureau, 701 Superior St., Wisconsin Dells, WI 53965. Phone 608-254-8088, or 800-22-DELLS.

150

Baraboo

Population 8,700. Location: Sauk County in south central Wisconsin. Access on U.S. Hwy 12, and on Wis. Hwy 33. Baraboo is about 40 miles north of Madison.

Baraboo High School

(now Baraboo Civic Center)
124 Second St.
Baraboo, WI 53913

Claude and Starck 1927

Open Monday-Friday 8:30-5, also evenings and weekends for special events. Phone 608-356-8333.

By 1927, the city high school built in 1906 was already too small, and local leaders contracted with Claude and Starck to design a new high school. (The 1906

Terra cotta ornament over the main entrance

structure was then to be converted to a junior high.)

The firm, well known in Wisconsin for its library designs (the 1903 Baraboo library was their first library commission), had also established a reputation as a designer of schools. Between 1905, when their first school project (since demolished) was built in Madison, and 1927, when Baraboo came to them, the firm had created some fifteen schools for Wisconsin communities.

Claude and Starck designed a simple tan brick three-story Prairie style structure. The key Prairie design elements are the thin brick pilasters that define the rows of windows on each side of the building, and the marvelous terra cotta ornament that bands the building along the flat roofline, along the windows, and around the doors. The three arched entrances are particularly ornate, with winged lions guarding each doorway. Historians have been unable to determine whether Claude and Starck created the terra cotta designs or ordered ready-made designs from an architectural decorating company.

The building was used as a high school until 1962, when it, in turn, was converted to a junior high. In 1977, the city took it over and remodeled it into a civic center for city offices, day care, senior citizen activities, theater groups, and the Chamber of Commerce.

The interior has been remodeled, but many classrooms remain in original condition, with wood molding and even original blackboards. The third-floor auditorium and the basement gymnasium are in near-original condition.

Getting there: Take Second Street east from Broadway (Business Hwy 12) in downtown Baraboo. The high school (now Civic Center) is on the corner of Second Street and Ash Street.

Also of Interest

The office of the Island Woolen Mill, an example of Prairie style industrial architecture, still stands at the west end of Second Avenue at the Baraboo River. (Note: In Baraboo, numbered streets go east and numbered avenues go west from Broadway, which is the north-south divide street.) The mill office was designed by Claude and Starck in 1917. The mills closed in 1949, and most of the buildings burned in 1969. The office is now owned by the city.

The classical Baraboo Public Library (1903), the first of Claude and Starck's many library designs, has been enlarged, but the original portion of the building is beautifully preserved. At Fourth Avenue and Birch Street just west of downtown.

The Al Ringling theater, an opulent 1915 imitation of a French opera house, is beautifully restored and used for films and live events. 136 Fourth Ave. on the courthouse square.

A historic walking tour booklet and a list of local historic markers is available at the Chamber of Commerce office in the Civic Center. The walking tour focuses on events and personalities rather than on architecture, but it does take you by the key Baraboo historic structures.

For General Travel Information

Contact the Baraboo Chamber of Commerce, 124 Second St., Baraboo, WI 53913. Phone 608-356-8333.

153

15 Reedsburg

Population 5,000. Location: Sauk County in south central Wisconsin. Access is on Wis. Hwys 23 and 33. Reedsburg is about 60 miles northwest of Madison.

Reedsburg Public Library
345 Vine St.
Reedsburg, WI 53959

Claude and Starck 1911

Open Monday-Thursday 10-8, Friday-Saturday 10-4; summer Saturdays 10-1. Phone 608-524-3316.

In 1898 a lecture by Miss Lutie Stearns of the State Library Commission inspired the civic leaders of Reedsburg to begin raising money for a library. Within a year, the Reedsburg Public Library was operating out of a back room on Main Street. Later, it was moved to a larger space in the (then) City Hall, but by 1911 it was clear that once again the library needed more room.

City leaders applied for a $10,000 Carnegie Foundation grant, which was approved in February, 1911. The Library Board turned to Claude and Starck, who had produced libraries for Baraboo, Evansville (see p. 141), Darlington, Monroe, and a number of other small Midwestern communities. The new Reedsburg Public Library was dedicated on January 1, 1912.

Claude and Starck created a "modern" design similar to the one they were completing for the city of Jefferson at the same time. The red brick and stucco building had a long pitched roof accented in the front by gables surmounting two sets of windows on either side of the vestibule entrance. Rows of windows on the other three sides were placed high on the wall to allow maximum interior wall space for book-shelves.

As with many of their libraries, both classical and Prairie styles, Claude and Starck designed a two-story building with a raised basement that housed a community room for public events, and a main floor that contained the library. Patrons entered at mid-level, halfway between the basement and the first floor.

The Reedsburg library had a fireplace, a delicate geometric design of leaded glass in the row of windows and in glass panels around the main entrance door, a half-hexagon librarian's desk, and built-in bookshelves and periodical racks.

Unfortunately, major alterations in the past few decades have drastically changed the building. The first was an extension of the building to one side. That addition retained the roofline, but the original side wall was removed and replaced with a new windowless side wall. The second addition was a connection to the new City Hall complex and a further enlargement of the library to the rear. This addition eliminated the rear windows and part of the rear wall. Finally, the roof over the entrance was changed from a flat roof to a gabled one. While this change is sympathetic to the feel of the building, it is clearly not what Claude and Starck designed.

Because of the alterations, the library has lost many important design elements. Fortunately, some examples of Claude and Starck's design remain, including the front windows, and those windows on one side, many of the original furnishings, and much of the original roofline with its projecting eaves and bands of decorative molding under the eaves.

Getting there: The library is on Vine Street, which is one block south of and parallel to Main Street (Wis. Hwy 23).

Also of Interest

The Reedsburg Historic Survey published "Reedsburg's Architectural Heritage," a booklet listing homes and commercial and public buildings of historic interest. The booklet contains explanations of architectural styles as well as maps locating buildings in the Park Street Historic District and the Main Street Historic District. Reedsburg has a particularly fine historic downtown area. The booklet is available at the public library for $2.50.

For General Travel Information

Contact the Reedsburg Chamber of Commerce, Box 142, Reedsburg, WI 53959-0142. Phone 608-524-2850.

Spring Green

Population 1,400. Location: Sauk County in south central Wisconsin. Forty miles west of Madison on U.S. Hwy 14, which runs east-west. Wis. Hwy 23 provides access from north and south.

The Taliesin Complex
Route 3 (Wis. Hwy 23)
Spring Green, WI 53588

Frank Lloyd Wright 1887-1959

The Taliesin Complex, which is three miles south of Spring Green on Wis. Hwy 23, includes Wright-designed buildings, other structures, and the 600-acre portion of the Jones Valley on which they are located.

Portions of the complex are open to the public:

Hillside School tours are offered daily from mid-April to late October. The 45-minute tours begin on the hour from 9 a.m. to 4 p.m. Admission is charged.

Taliesin house tours take visitors into Taliesin, Wright's home. The three-hour tour includes refreshments and a chance to talk with long-time members of the Taliesin Fellowship. Tours are offered on a limited basis in summer and early fall. Reservations are required. Admission is charged.

Taliesin walking tours take visitors past the major buildings of the Taliesin complex, including the Romeo and Juliet tower, Taliesin, and Midway Farm. The one-and-one-half hour walking tours leave Hillside School daily at 10:30 a.m. from early June to September. Admission is charged.

For tour information and reservations, contact Taliesin at 608-588-2511.

The Jones Valley

The 600-acre Taliesin complex straddles Wright's home valley, where he worked summers on the farms of his Lloyd Jones uncles. The complex includes the living and working quarters of the Taliesin Fellowship and Taliesin Associated Architects, as well as farmland and a pond created by the damming of Jones Creek.

A tour of Taliesin is incomplete without taking time to look at the landscape Wright created, a landscape which he considered integral to his overall architectural design.

The valley in the early 20th century was home to a number of Lloyd Jones farms, as well as Unity Chapel, the adjoining cemetery, and Hillside School. The land was largely in field, pasture, and woodlot, though fields were smaller than the ones we see today, and there were more fencerows.

When Wright arrived in 1911 and began building Taliesin, he also dammed Jones Creek to create a pond. He built a powerhouse next to the dam, and for years was the only local resident with electricity (though reports are that the amount generated was barely enough to light a few bulbs).

Over the years, Wright inherited or purchased much of the land in the valley and the area upstream along the Wisconsin River. Wright had many unfulfilled ideas for this land, including a Taliesin Parkway along County Highway C, and a Taliesin airport on the flat land north of Highway 14. He did raise cattle for a time on the land that is now the Springs golf course. Wright, and the Taliesin Fellowship, his successor in ownership, eventually sold that land, while retaining the property in Jones Valley.

In 1945, Wright added a second upper dam on Jones Creek to provide a pond below Midway Farm. The main entrance to Taliesin at that time was from Highway 23 across the upper dam and up the hill to the house. The upper dam was removed because it caused water problems for the upstream landowner. The lower dam and powerhouse were washed out in a flood, and only the dam was rebuilt. The pond is today the site of parties and the annual June 8 (Wright's birthday) fireworks display.

Wright was constantly working to beautify the landscape. He and the apprentices planted trees and flowers along the roads. He insisted on removal of billboards and unnecessary road signs. He convinced the phone company to remove its lines along Highway 23 and put them through the woods on a ridge above the valley. He refused to allow public power at Taliesin because he wouldn't allow overhead power lines on the property. (In addition to the meager electricity from the dam, Wright used generators for electricity.) Wright even began strip-cropping and contour plowing as early as 1918, although it is not clear whether he did this for conservation purposes or for aesthetic reasons.

The Jones Valley today looks much as it did in the 1950s. The fields of Taliesin are still cultivated, though livestock are no longer housed on the property.

Taliesin III from the east. The studio wing joins the living quarters at the right.

Taliesin I
Frank Lloyd Wright 1911

Taliesin II
Frank Lloyd Wright 1914

Taliesin III
Frank Lloyd Wright 1925

159

State Historical Society of Wisconsin

Taliesin I courtyard, about 1913

Wright broke his ties to Oak Park in 1909 and sailed to Europe with Mamah Borthwick Cheney. When he returned in 1910 he spent a few months in Oak Park, but he was a social outcast with virtually no commissions and he soon left for Spring Green, where he had never lived, but where many childhood (and adult) summers had been spent with his Lloyd Jones relatives, who still dominated the valley. Wright had already left his mark on the valley. Unity Chapel, Hillside School, the Romeo and Juliet windmill, and Tan-y-deri, home of his sister Helen Porter and her husband, all stood within a short distance of the hill on which Taliesin, his new home, was rising.

Wright had designed a summer house for his mother to be built on the hill, which she owned. When Wright felt obliged to leave Oak Park, she offered him the site, staying instead at Hillside School with her sisters Nell and Jane.

Wright redesigned and considerably enlarged the planned home, adding a studio, caretaker's quarters, a dairy, a dovecote (a sort of pen for domestic pigeons), and a chicken coop. His quest for self-sufficiency included damming Jones Creek and building a powerhouse at the base of the hill on which Taliesin—Welsh for "shining brow"—was taking shape. The main entrance to Taliesin I was from Highway 23 (the stone entrance markers are still next to the road) up the hill into a porte-cochere in the courtyard adjoining the living quarters.

He took Mamah Cheney to the unfinished Taliesin in August, 1911, after she obtained a divorce. Though they would live mainly at Taliesin, Wright maintained a Chicago office and carried on his architectural practice from two locations.

Perhaps because Wright had virtually no work at the time, or perhaps because he so loved the valley, he poured his creative energy into the home he was building for Mamah. Taliesin inspired some of the most eloquent passages in his autobiography: "This hill on which Taliesin now stands as 'brow' was one of my favorite places when as a boy looking for pasque flowers I went there in March sun while snow still streaked the hillsides...I knew well that no house should ever be on a hill or on anything. It should be of the hill. Belonging to it. Hill and house should live together each the happier for the other... How quiet and strong the rock-ledge masses looked with the dark red cedars and white birches, there, above the green slopes. They were all part of the countenance of southern Wisconsin. I wished to be part of my beloved southern Wisconsin, too...A stone quarry there on another hill a mile away was where the yellow sand-limestone, uncovered, lay in strata like outcropping ledges in facades of the hills. The look of it was what I wanted for such masses as would rise from these native slopes." (*An Autobiography*, Frank Lloyd Wright, Duell, Sloan and Pearce, 1943.)

With the help of local farmers and craftsmen, Wright built Taliesin, a roughly L-shaped series of limestone and cypress buildings hugging the hillside some sixty feet above the valley floor. Wright explains in his autobiography, "Taliesin was to be an abstract combination of stone and wood as they naturally met in the aspect of the hills around about. The lines of the hills were the lines of the roofs, the slopes of the hills their slopes, the plastered surfaces of the light wood-walls, set back into shade beneath broad eaves, were like the flat stretches of sand in the river below and the same in color, for that is where the material that covered them came from."

In August, 1914, the greatest tragedy of Wright's life occurred at Taliesin while he was working on construction of Midway Gardens in Chicago. Mamah, her two children, and a group of workers and their children were eating lunch when a servant set fire to the dining room area, then brutally murdered seven people—Mamah, her children, the son of a worker, and three workers—as they tried to flee the flames. The living quarters of Taliesin burned before neighbors could stop the fire.

Wright buried Mamah in a simple grave in the Lloyd Jones cemetery next to Unity Chapel. He planted a pine tree at the head of her grave. The servant was arrested, but committed suicide without ever explaining his actions.

161

This part of Taliesin was not touched by the two fires. It has been remodeled into offices and apartments.

The fire did not damage Wright's drawings, plans, art work and other materials in the studio wing. He immediately set to work building Taliesin II, making it larger than its predecessor, adding rooms for his mother and aunts Nell and Jane, and expanding his studio. It was completed in 1915.

Possibly because Wright spent much of the time between 1915 and 1925 in Japan and California, and so was not at Taliesin very often, Taliesin II is considerably less well documented and is little discussed in books about Wright's work.

In 1925, when faulty wiring caused another fire that destroyed the living quarters of Taliesin II, Wright was divorcing Miriam Noel, his second wife, and was involved with Olgivanna Milanov Hinzenburg. Olgivanna soon became Wright's third wife, and Taliesin became their headquarters.

Taliesin III, which rose from the rubble of the second fire, continued to grow and change throughout Wright's life. Taliesin III, the building we see today, contains 37,000 square feet housing living quarters, guest rooms and apartments, Wright's studio and offices, storage facilities, and farm buildings.

State Historical Society of Wisconsin

Living room of Taliesin III in the late 1950s

The house still clings to the hillside in the same location as Taliesin I. The most famous and striking feature of Taliesin III is the living room. Olgivanna asked for a two-story living room, so Wright expanded Taliesin upward, changing it from a single story home to a multi-level one. With its rows of windows overlooking the valley, and clerestories providing light from above, the peaked ceiling with bands of wood molding, the irregular horizontal limestone strata of the walls, and the narrow birdwalk jutting forty feet out from the living room over the treetops, the dramatic room is a constant visual delight.

Access to the living room is through a low entrance foyer, which also connects to the Wrights' bedrooms, his study, and guest rooms. The second story above houses guest rooms and what used to be their daughter Iovanna's apartment when she was at home. Beneath the main floor is a wing housing apartments and guest rooms.

Access to Wright's studio is through a covered breezeway. The space was originally used by Wright and his apprentices, draftsmen and helpers. It now houses

163

Taliesin III from the southwest

business offices for the Frank Lloyd Wright Foundation. Housed in the same wing are apartments and living quarters converted over the years from chicken coops, pig pens, and the dovecote.

Every year, Wright changed Taliesin, as he did Hillside School and practically every other building he had any control over. Interiors were continually redecorated and rearranged. Farm and storage areas at Taliesin were remodeled into living areas. Farm buildings were added and some were eventually converted to living spaces. Wright also designed buildings for the nearby hillside that were never built.

Taliesin is one of the masterworks of modern architecture. It has been nominated as a United Nations World Heritage site. Taliesin is Wright at his best. The building accomplishes everything he preached: It fuses building and site through the use of natural materials—wood, stone and plaster—in a way that complements the hillside rather than dominating it. It is sited to provide lovely vistas of the valley and the river. The stone terraces and floors, the large expanses of glass and the overhanging eaves merge outdoors and indoors. It breaks open the box (it is difficult to decide exactly how many rooms Taliesin has because they all flow from one to the next). It is constantly changing due to the interplay of light and shadow as the sun moves through the sky. To study Taliesin is to begin to understand Wright's principles of organic architecture.

164

Hillside School today. Romeo and Juliet tower in the background.

Hillside School

Frank Lloyd Wright 1887 (Home building, demolished 1950)
Frank Lloyd Wright 1902 (Hillside School, still in use)

Wright's aunts Nell and Jane Lloyd Jones began the Hillside Home School in 1886 on the site of their family farm. As Wright recalls in his autobiography, "When working for Silsbee in Chicago I had made the amateurish plans for the very first school buildings; Cramer the local contractor had built them." (*An Autobiography*, Frank Lloyd Wright, Duell, Sloan and Pearce, 1943.)

The 1887 Hillside Home building is considered Wright's first independent commission. The twenty-year-old novice produced a shingle-style building that looks much like Silsbee's work—not surprising given Wright's inexperience and his professed admiration for his then-employer.

The Home building was up the hill from the location of the present Hillside School. Originally, the Home building was the school's central structure. The thirty to forty boarding students (ages five to eighteen) lived on the second and third floors and the living areas and library occupied the first floor.

165

State Historical Society of Wisconsin

Hillside Home building—Wright's first independent commission

By 1900, the aunts needed more space for their nationally-recognized progressive school. They again called on their nephew, who by this time was well established in his architectural practice in Oak Park and who had taken Silsbee, Sullivan, and other influences, melded them, added his own ideas, and produced buildings unlike anything seen before. The 1902 Hillside School was one of his first masterpieces.

Wright designed an L-shaped building of native sandstone and oak. The longer wing (at that time) faced south. On one end of this wing was the three-story gymnasium, with running track and spectator seating. On the other end was the three-story assembly room, with the library housed in the balcony. Connecting the gym and assembly room was a two-story row of classrooms, the carpentry shop, and principal's room.

State Historical Society of Wisconsin

Original Hillside school—gymnasium in foreground

A second story bridge over the driveway connected the main wing to the smaller wing, which housed art and science classrooms.

Hillside School closed in 1917, and within a few years both aunts were dead. They left the land and buildings to their nephew Frank. The buildings stood empty for more than a decade.

In 1928, Wright developed a plan to refurbish and enlarge Hillside School for a proposed Hillside Home School of Applied Arts, at which he, Olgivanna, and others would teach architecture, painting, sculpture, music, drama, and photography. The 1929 stock market crash put an end to the plan.

In 1932, though, he and Olgivanna began the Taliesin Fellowship, and his long-planned expansion of Hillside School began to take shape.

The newly-arrived apprentices built the drafting room and added dorm rooms to the Hillside School under Wright's supervision. They also converted the gym to a theater. Wright intended to incorporate the Home building into the planned complex, but found only limited use for it and finally demolished it.

167

State Historical Society of Wisconsin

Gymnasium in the original Hillside school

Hillside School became the center of the Fellowship. Apprentices lived and worked there. The classrooms of earlier days were converted into a kitchen and dining hall and offices. The theater was the scene of regular parties, theatricals and musical events put on by the Fellowship. And, of course, much of the architectural production of the Fellowship came from the drafting room.

The drafting room is one of Wright's most inventive interiors. He called its intricate triangular network of beams and supports resting on triangular iron cups an "abstract forest." Daylight filters into the "forest" through clerestories, constantly changing the look and feel of the room. From plywood, a new material he took to immediately, Wright created the drafting room floor by cutting strips about one and a half inches thick and laying them on edge to expose the layering. The effect is stunning.

In 1952, Wright and several apprentices were raking and burning leaves when the wind carried embers under the eaves of the theater, causing a fire that destroyed

Brent Nicastro

Drafting studio—Hillside School

169

Hillside Theater

Brent Nicastro

much of the wing.

Wright eagerly took the opportunity to rebuild the theater in a manner more to his liking. The current theater, with its low foyer opening onto the semi-circular seating area, dates from this rebuilding. From the assembly room, through the dining area and into the theater is now one open space of varying levels. When the theater curtains and other screens are removed, you can see from one end to the other. The theater curtain, a gift to Wright from Mrs. Wright and the apprentices, is an abstraction of a Wisconsin summer landscape, with green hills, red barns, gray storm clouds, and golden wheat fields.

Romeo and Juliet Windmill

Frank Lloyd Wright 1896

    This wooden tower is the oldest existing Wright building in Wisconsin. He designed it to pump water from an adjoining hilltop reservoir for Hillside School.

    The sixty-foot-high interlocking octagon (Juliet) and diamond (Romeo) tower set on a stone foundation is unique as a windmill design. Romeo contained the windmill and its drive apparatus, and shorter Juliet housed a stairway to an observation deck.

171

Romeo and Juliet was Wright's first use of two concepts he developed further as he continued his architectural practice: The tower was designed much like a barrel—with no internal cross supports. The shingled skin of the tower, and its partial flooring every ten feet from bottom to top, held the tower in place. Wright also determined that two interlocking geometric forms (octagon and diamond in this case) were stronger together than if each stood separately.

Wright in his autobiography wrote, "...the thing is just a sort of big octagonal wood pipe, 4x4 posts at each corner, boards nailed around to the posts, inside and outside. Then all shingled...The whole thing is just like a barrel, only the staves run around across instead of running up and down." (*An Autobiography*, Frank Lloyd Wright, Duell, Sloan and Pearce, 1943.)

Wright's design caused considerable local and family consternation because it was so completely different from the ubiquitous steel frame windmill towers that dotted the farms of the Midwest and Great Plains (and which would have cost perhaps $250, instead of the $950 Wright's design cost).

The Lloyd Jones uncles, practical and frugal, wanted aunts Nell and Jane to build a cheaper, and guaranteed, steel frame windmill. So did Cramer, the local contractor who had built the Hillside School buildings Wright designed in 1887. The aunts wanted something artistic as well as practical, however, and they always wanted to assist their nephew in his architectural practice.

But, worried about Cramer's opinion, Nell and Jane wired Wright in Oak Park, "Cramer says windmill tower sure to fall. Are you sure it will stand?" Wright wired back, "Build it." They did.

The windmill stood untouched until 1938, when Taliesin apprentices repaired it and replaced the original shingle siding with horizontal cypress board and batten.

In 1991, the old windmill, not used for decades, was finally about to succumb to the ravages of rodents, insects and the Wisconsin climate. As part of the long-range effort to restore Taliesin buildings, in a $250,000 renovation the tower was dismantled, restored and rebuilt, and many of the trees that had grown up on the formerly bare hilltop over the years were removed.

172

Tan-y-deri

Frank Lloyd Wright 1907

Wright had two younger sisters, Jane and Maginel. Jane married Canadian businessman Andrew Porter and moved to Toronto. But she, like so many of the Lloyd Jones clan, wanted to return to the family valley.

Her husband, who carried on several businesses throughout his life, was pretty much able to live anywhere, so he agreed to move to Spring Green.

Jane asked her brother to produce a house for her small family (the Porters had a son, Franklin). Tan-y-deri, which means "under the oaks" in Welsh, was based on Wright's 1907 *Ladies Home Journal* article that proposed a "Fireproof House for $5000" (see p. 5).

Wright did several versions of his *Ladies Home Journal* plan, including homes in Mason City, Iowa, and La Grange, Illinois. Tan-y-deri is the only Wisconsin example of Wright's use of this design.

173

Living quarters adjoining Tan-y-deri. A remodeled cow shed and chicken coop.

Instead of concrete (the reason the $5000 house is fireproof), however, the Porter's house is a wood frame structure with shingle siding. The hipped roof with overhanging eaves and the diamond-pane leaded glass windows were common elements in Wright designs of the time.

The interior of the square home has four bedrooms upstairs, all opening on a central foyer. Downstairs the living and dining rooms wrap around the central fireplace. Both rooms open on the porch, with its spectacular view over the Lloyd Jones valley. (Tan-y-deri is the best place to watch storms roll in across the valley, according to current members of the Fellowship.)

Wright sited the house on the side of a hill below the Romeo and Juliet tower. On the other side of the hill were the buildings of Hillside School.

In 1914, when Mamah Cheney and six others were murdered at Taliesin, the bodies were brought to Tan-y-deri. In 1925, when fire again leveled the living quarters of Taliesin II, Wright and his wife Olgivanna moved into Tan-y-deri while Taliesin was rebuilt.

The relationship between the Porters and Wright was not always smooth. They once sued him over money he owed them for farm products, and Frank and Jane would

Cottage adjoining
Tan-y-deri. A
remodeled tool shed.

regularly have fights and not speak to each other for months.

Jane Porter outlived her husband by some years, and when she died in the mid-1950s, her son Franklin turned Tan-y-deri over to the Taliesin Fellowship. It has been used ever since to house Fellowship members and guests.

The house has been slightly remodeled to better accommodate several families. An exterior entrance to the second floor was added at the rear, and the basement was converted into a separate apartment.

The small cottages just down the hill from Tan-y-deri began as outbuildings for the Porter's farm. The one closest to Tan-y-deri was originally the chicken coop and cow shed. When the Fellowship began to grow, apprentices remodeled the coop and shed into a small apartment. They converted the shed into a kitchen, added an area above the shed for bedrooms, and converted the chicken coop into a living room. They also built the obligatory stone fireplace. For many years the structure was called the "engineer's cottage" because engineer Mendal Glickman, who worked on many of Wright's major projects, spent summers in the cottage. Today a senior Taliesin architect and his family occupy the cottage during the summer.

The smaller cottage was originally a tool shed. Apprentices converted it into a cozy two-level, one-room cottage. Because it is so small, it is occupied by only one person.

The cottages were not designed by any one person. They grew as apprentices had time to work, or as living space was needed.

The Fellowship plans to winterize the cottages for eventual year-round use.

175

Midway farm. Enos Lloyd Jones house visible behind silo at right.

Midway Farm

Frank Lloyd Wright 1938-1947

Originally, the farm buildings associated with Taliesin were on the hillside behind Wright's home. Hillside School also had a barn. From the time he first returned to the valley in 1911, Wright always tried to maintain a self-sufficient operation with a productive farm.

As the Taliesin Fellowship grew, chicken coops were converted into apprentice housing, and Wright felt the need for a new set of farm buildings away from the living quarters and architectural design studios. He put the new buildings midway between Taliesin and Hillside School.

The barn, a long, low, wood and limestone structure, housed dairy cattle, calves, horses (Wright enjoyed riding), and feed. Pig pens and chicken coops were nearby, as was a machine shed. In 1947, he added the limestone tower of the creamery, its spire he claimed was his "monument to the Guernsey teat." Wright carried his sense of design to his farming operation. He wouldn't have black and white cattle, insisting on brown and white ones because they seemed more like deer in a park. He also insisted on red

**The Creamery at
Midway farm**

chickens because, he said, white chickens look like newspaper blowing around the barnyard.

Taliesin apprentices, neighboring farmers, and hired herdsmen tended the cows, chickens, and pigs, and grew vegetables for the Fellowship and hay and corn for

177

the livestock. The Fellowship kept about forty cows, and produced enough fruits and vegetables to can hundreds of quarts of tomatoes and other produce to take on the annual trip to winter quarters at Taliesin West in Scottsdale, Arizona.

At the north end of the Midway barn are a row of tiny apartments, used originally by herdsmen, now used by Taliesin associates and guests. The Fellowship no longer keeps livestock, and the corn fields are tended by neighboring farmers.

The barn has deteriorated and is now stabilized by temporary structural supports. The Fellowship intends to determine an appropriate use for the building and eventually renovate it.

Wright's Uncle Enos Lloyd Jones had a small four-room house near where Wright built the dam on Jones Creek. In 1933, Wright and the apprentices moved the house to its present location just up the hill behind Midway farm. Apprentices have completely remodeled it over the years, adding the standard stone fireplace, removing walls and redesigning rooms in the interior, and refinishing the exterior. The Fellowship recently built a small apartment adjoining the house. The house and apartment are used for summer housing for Taliesin associates and guests.

Unity Chapel
County Hwy. T
Spring Green

Joseph Lyman Silsbee 1886

Chapel open for services and special events only. Adjoining cemetery open daily.

J.L. Silsbee was Wright's second employer (after Allan Conover), but even before Wright began his formal position with Silsbee, he worked on this Lloyd Jones family chapel.

Silsbee was a friend of Wright's uncle Jenkin Lloyd Jones, who was a Unitarian minister in Chicago, and Silsbee designed All Souls Church for Jenkin in 1885. Shortly thereafter, Silsbee designed this small chapel for Jenkin's home valley.

Frank Lloyd Wright's rendering of the chapel appeared in the All Souls annual for 1886. "A boy architect belonging to the family,"—19-year-old Frank—also "looked after" work on the chapel interior, according to a contemporary Unitarian publication.

179

The chapel, typical of Silsbee's work, is an L-shaped shingle and sandstone structure with a hipped roof crowned by a narrow tower. The Wright-supervised interior is simple, consisting of an entry, a kitchen (now a storage room), and a large meeting room that could be divided by a curtain into two sections.

The chapel played an important role in Wright's life. Not only did he worship there, but most of his Lloyd Jones relatives were buried in the chapel cemetery. Through the years, many family members and close associates were interred in the peaceful churchyard.

The chapel and cemetery were important enough to Wright that in 1957 he designed a second chapel and a burial site for Taliesin associates to be adjacent to Unity Chapel and the family cemetery. The design was not executed.

Buried in the chapel cemetery are Wright's mother, his aunts Nell and Jane, his sister Maginel, and numerous aunts, uncles, cousins, and other relatives. Five of his children—Lloyd, John, Catherine, Frances, and Robert—lie here. At the foot of a pine tree planted by Wright is the grave of Mamah Borthwick Cheney, now marked by a simple limestone slab. Wright's longtime secretary Eugene Masselink is buried next to Wright's original grave.

Wright died in April, 1959, in Arizona. Wesley Peters and other Taliesin associates drove the body back to Spring Green and buried Wright in the family plot next to Unity Chapel. When she died in 1985, Olgivanna Wright's will specified that Wright's body be removed to Taliesin West, to be cremated and interred with her. The body was moved, and Wright's original gravestone, still in place, now marks an empty grave.

Getting there: Take Wis. Hwy 23 south three miles from Spring Green. Turn east on County Hwy T.

Also of Interest

A few hundred yards farther along Hwy T is Aldebaran, one of the original Lloyd Jones farms. It has long been believed that this farm was the one where young Frank spent his summers doing farm work for his uncles. (Another candidate for the summer work farm has emerged south on Highway 23 past the Hillside School.) Aldebaran has been heavily remodeled and now provides visitor housing. Phone 608-588-2951.

The Spring Green Restaurant
Hwy 23
Spring Green, WI 53588

Frank Lloyd Wright 1953

Open daily for lunch and dinner. Phone 608-588-2571.

This lovely spot overlooking the Wisconsin River at the intersection of Highway 23 and County Highway C is within sight of Taliesin. Wright was particularly annoyed that an unattractive establishment called Bridge Lunch occupied this premier location. As he did with much of the land in the area, he tried to buy it. For years he had no luck. Finally, the owners sold out.

Wright had designed a number of different buildings that could have fit the site, but by the time he actually bought it, he had decided on a restaurant, and he intended to have the Fellowship members involved in its operation.

Work didn't begin until 1957, and progressed slowly. When Wright died in 1959, the restaurant was still unfinished. Work didn't resume until the mid-1960s, and

181

**Spring Green
Restaurant—
main entrance**

the restaurant opened, somewhat changed from Wright's original design, in 1967. The Fellowship's leaders were wise enough to know they were architects, not cooks, so they turned the restaurant over to the Wisconsin River Development Corporation, as the first building of a planned resort complex in the area. Also to be built were downhill ski facilities, a golf course, and both permanent and vacation housing. (Some facilities have been completed over the years by a succession of developers.)

The restaurant Wright designed was intended to provide a striking view of the river and at the same time to be, in itself, a striking view from the river and from the Highway 23 bridge. Steel trusses from an aircraft carrier support the narrow, 300-foot-long building. It extends along the side of the hill, supported on limestone piers that raise it to take advantage of the stunning views. The octagonal section at one end houses offices.

Facing the river a row of windows runs the length of the building. On the hill side the limestone walls rise to a row of narrow clerestories.

Entry is from the rear through a low passage into the open dining room, with its high, peaked ceiling. Or, turn left from the entry and wind through a narrow passage into the bar, where the low ceiling and massive stone fireplace provide a feeling of intimacy. The view from the bar at sunset is spectacular.

The furniture in the restaurant was designed by Olgivanna Wright.

Getting there: The restaurant is two and a half miles south of Spring Green at the intersection of Hwy 23 and County Hwy C.

Wyoming Valley School

6306 Wis. Hwy 23
Town of Wyoming
Spring Green, WI 53588

Frank Lloyd Wright 1956

Closed and in private ownership; outside can be viewed at any time.

In early 1956, the citizens of the Town of Wyoming voted to consolidate the community's six remaining one-room schools. Town officials asked Frank Lloyd Wright to design the new school.

Wright was obviously anxious to take on the commission. Even though he was heavily committed to the Guggenheim Museum in New York, the Greek Orthodox Church outside Milwaukee, the Marin County Center outside San Francisco, and many other residential and institutional projects, Wright agreed to donate his design to the town. In addition, he contributed $7000 toward the final $52,000 cost of the school, and he bought an additional two and a half acres to enlarge the site to more than five

183

acres, which he considered necessary to properly site the building he envisioned.

Perhaps Wright was pleased to at last be recognized by a Wisconsin government, even a small township government, since his other designs (for a civic center in Madison, for bridges, for a Milwaukee County museum and library) for government projects had been rejected. Or perhaps he was trying to make peace with the town after his 1954 threat to burn Taliesin and leave the state if the town didn't give him a property tax break for the Hillside School. (He claimed it deserved an education exemption; the town said it was a profit-making venture. The courts ruled in favor of the town.)

In any event, Wright produced his third school. (The others are Hillside School at Taliesin and a girl's school in Japan. He also designed an entire college campus in Florida.) The Wyoming Valley school is a simple, open and airy structure of concrete block with wood trim and poured concrete floors. The building is essentially an elongated hexagon. A raised roof in the center echoes the building's shape and provides overhead lighting through a ring of clerestory windows.

The interior is divided into two sections by a central hall that runs the width of the building. One section contains two classrooms, the other an assembly room. A massive concrete block core with two fireplaces, one facing the central hall and one facing into the assembly room, is the focal point of the building. Small side extensions from the basic floor plan contain a kitchen, restrooms, a teachers' room, and storage areas. With rows of windows along the classroom walls and the clerestories above, the building needs virtually no artificial light during the day.

Small touches show Wright's genius. Mahogany-faced beams rising from opposite walls to cross in an X pattern, and the ceilings—low at the outer walls then stepping up toward the clerestories in the center of the structure—make the building continually interesting and create a changing play of light and shadow as the sun moves across the sky.

Work on the school began in spring, 1957, with Marshall Erdman, one of Wright's favorite contractors (see pp. 106 and 128), handling construction work. The building was dedicated in January, 1958. Forty-three students in grades one through eight, and their two teachers, began classes immediately. As Wright had predicted, the school was instantly popular with local residents as well as the students. Local civic and volunteer groups often used the assembly room, which Wright had dedicated to the memory of his mother Anna and his aunts Nell and Jane.

In 1988, the school fell victim to further school consolidation, and it was sold at auction for $305,000 to a Chicago developer who has other interests in the valley. The building is vacant while he determines a suitable use. He intends to open it to the public.

Getting there: The school is four miles south of Spring Green on Wis. Hwy 23.

Also of Interest

Though no Wright designs were ever built in Spring Green itself, the work of Taliesin Associated Architects (TAA) is represented. The Valley Bank Spring Green, at the corner of East Jefferson and North Worcester in downtown Spring Green was designed by William Wesley Peters. Also at that intersection, the medical office across Worcester Street from the bank is a TAA design, as is the pharmacy across Jefferson Street from the bank. Peters also designed St. John's Catholic Church, on East Daley Street between North Lexington and North Washington just a few blocks from downtown. TAA also designed the buildings of the new resort complex adjoining the Springs golf course off County Highway C near the Spring Green Restaurant.

For General Travel Information

Contact the Spring Green Chamber of Commerce, Box 3, Spring Green, WI 53588. Phone 608-588-2042.

17 Richland Center

Population 5,000. Location: Richland County in southwest Wisconsin. Access on U.S. Hwy 14. Richland Center is about 60 miles west of Madison, and about 20 miles west of Spring Green.

The A.D. German Warehouse
300 South Church St.
Richland Center, WI 53581

Frank Lloyd Wright 1915

Open Tuesday-Sunday, May 1-November 1, some winter weekends. Phone 608-647-2808.

Albert Dell German (pronounced "Jarman") was born in 1875 into a Welsh immigrant family in rural Richland County. He went into business in Richland Center

186

and prospered as a wholesaler of cement, coal, hay, and grain.

In 1916 he announced to the local newspaper that he was soon to build a Frank Lloyd Wright-designed warehouse on a lot adjacent to his home on South Church Street. The building would provide storage for wholesale goods and would also include a tea room, retail shops, an art gallery, and a Frank Lloyd Wright exhibit. The entire building, said German, would cost $30,000.

Local lore has it that German got a Wright-designed building because Wright was deep in debt to the merchant from purchases to keep nearby Taliesin going. German despaired of collecting cash and settled for plans for his new warehouse.

Work didn't begin until the fall of 1917, and continued sporadically for nearly four years. By 1919 the unfinished building had cost $125,000, and German was sinking into financial trouble due to a fire, loses on sugar speculation during World War I, and other setbacks. In 1921 he boarded up the windows and unfinished front entrance and halted work.

German's money pit is unique among Wright's works. It is the only warehouse he ever designed. It is also the first of his "Mayan" buildings, a group of fortress-like structures with few windows, solid walls, and heavy tops. Wright developed this form mainly in his houses for southern California, and then dropped it from his repertoire by the late 1920s.

The warehouse is a four-story brick and concrete box broken only by narrow slit windows. Interior concrete columns, not the brick walls, support the weight of the building. A small, two-story annex, added on the second version of the design, was to be a music room and family area for German, who lived next door.

Of the four floors, the second and third are identical, open storage areas. The fourth floor, which was designed for cold storage, is also open, but instead of brick interior and exterior walls, it is enclosed by a cast-in-place concrete frieze. The frieze is interrupted by 54 narrow windows that define each unit of the abstract design. The frieze rises above the level of the flat roof to form a parapet, intended to enclose a roof garden.

The first floor was designed for offices (and, presumably, the gallery, shops, tea room, and Wright exhibit). It was to have large windows adjoining the Church Street entrance.

The walls are faced on the exterior with red brick and on the interior with yellow brick. Every fourth exterior brick is placed sideways as a "tie brick." The walls are one brick length thick, so the interior yellow brick walls are broken by the regular pattern of the ends of the red tie bricks.

Detail of the cast concrete frieze on the fourth floor

The concrete projections at each corner of the warehouse were intended to hold flagpoles or lights.

German lost the still-boarded-up warehouse in 1932 due to unpaid taxes. He never lost faith in Wright, however, and in 1935 convinced several partners to join him in a new warehouse scheme. Wright devised plans to convert the fourth floor into eight small apartments, to develop the rooftop terrace, and to open the first floor as a restaurant. (A use for the second and third floors wasn't specified.) Financing couldn't be found, though, and the project got no further than Wright's drawings.

German died in 1945, never having used his warehouse.

Others did use it for more than forty years, however. It passed through a series of owners and a variety of uses, including a temporary storage building for local merchants, and a bowling pin factory. In the 1950s, local authorities fitted it out as a fallout shelter.

In the 1970s, its owners, hoping to capitalize on the building as a Frank Lloyd Wright design, completed the main entrance essentially according to Wright's original intention. The current owners have a gift shop and Wright exhibit, and intend to open a restaurant.

Getting there: South Church Street is U.S. Hwy 14 in downtown Richland Center.

Also of Interest

Richland Center has two buildings designed by Percy Bentley. The Fred Pratt house, 314 North Central Ave., is a dark brown brick Prairie style home designed in 1919. The Richland Center City Hall and Auditorium, 182 North Central Ave., is a classical style edifice designed in 1911.

The warehouse, the Bentley buildings and two dozen other historic structures are located within easy walking distance in the city. A walking tour pamphlet, "Historical and Architectural Tour of Richland Center," can be obtained at the warehouse or from the Chamber of Commerce.

For General Travel Information

Contact the Richland Area Chamber of Commerce, Box 128, Richland Center, WI 53581. Phone 608-647-6205, or 800-422-1318.

18

Lancaster

Population 4,200. Location: Grant County in southwest Wisconsin. From Madison, take U.S. Hwy 18 west to Fennimore, then U.S. Hwy 61 south to Lancaster. Wis. Hwy 81 runs east-west through Lancaster, joining U.S. Hwy 151 in Platteville, 15 miles to the southeast.

Lancaster Municipal Building

206 S. Madison St.
Lancaster, WI 53813

Claude and Starck 1919

City Hall open during business hours, some evenings for public meetings. Phone 608-723-4246. Grantland Theater open throughout the week for evening and matinee performances. Phone 608-723-7469.

Lancaster Municipal building—detail of theater facade

After World War I, everyone in Lancaster agreed on the need for city offices and a fire station to replace the one demolished before the war, but debate raged in the building committee about the wisdom of including a municipal theater in the plans. One side argued that an elaborate facility would be a white elephant, but they were outvoted by civic boosters who wanted a local showpiece.

The $130,000 building was completed in 1922, three years after Claude and Starck first drew up the plans. The amber brick complex, joined two-story rectangles with a one-story extension for the fire station, is the only remaining Prairie School building of its kind in Wisconsin.

The building has a number of Prairie characteristics—the horizontal rows of windows, the simple lines adorned with intricate terra cotta ornament, and the geometric pattern of the leaded glass windows in the theater and surrounding the main door to City Hall.

The City Hall half of the complex has been partially remodeled, but the second floor meeting room remains essentially as Claude and Starck designed it, with folding

191

wood room dividers, and oak moldings that unite the windows and doors, tying the room together into a single unit. In addition to modernizing most offices and remodeling the basement for office space, the fire station was moved to a new building adjacent to the theater and the old firehouse space converted to a senior center.

The restored Grantland Theater is again an opulent local showcase, with neoclassical plaster ornament and friezes painted ivory, gold, and blue. These days, the theater is devoted to the latest movies.

Getting there: The Municipal Building is on the southeast corner of the Courthouse Square.

The Kinney House
474 N. Fillmore St.

Frank Lloyd Wright 1951

Private home. Not open to the public.

After Margaret and Pat Kinney married and settled in Lancaster, where Pat practiced law, they decided to build a home. Both were familiar with the work of Frank Lloyd Wright. (Margaret had worked with a children's theater group organized by Wright's sister Jane Porter, and so knew Wright personally.) They called on the master to design a home suited to the 2.5 acres of hilltop cornfield they had purchased at the edge of town.

Using topographic maps and photos of the site, Wright designed the home to get maximum benefit from its location while providing privacy on the street side. Wright used a four-foot-long diamond as his design grid, producing a hexagon containing the living-dining area, kitchen and master bedroom, with a bedroom wing attached to one side of the hexagon. All angles in the house are either 60 degrees or 120 degrees.

The Kinneys asked Wright for two bedrooms instead of the one he had designed in the bedroom wing. "We have three children," they explained. "That's too many," Wright replied, but he did revise the plan to include a second bedroom.

Large windows on three sides of the hexagon afford spectacular views across the surrounding hills, while the street side of the house shows passersby only stone walls and a row of clerestories.

In the center of the hexagon the limestone kitchen-fireplace core rises two stories to a skylight. The ceiling slopes upward to the skylight, giving a "wigwam" feel to this central living area.

Given a limited budget—roughly $15,000—Wright suggested the home be built of concrete block, the cheapest building material. Pat Kinney, however, wanted a stone house, and to keep costs down he quarried all the tan limestone himself at nearby quarries. Using mainly a crowbar, he pried loose some 300 tons of limestone for the walls, floor, and the footings on which the house rests.

Since none of the local builders wanted to bid on the house, Kinney scoured southern Wisconsin to find masons, carpenters, a heating contractor (the design called for in-floor radiant heating), and an electrician who would work on the house.

Construction took more than a year, with Kinney quarrying frantically to stay ahead of the masons' demand. The outer walls are double thickness—a layer of stone, an air space, and another layer of stone. During construction, the electrician had to come nearly every day and add to the conduit in the air space between the walls after the masons had finished their day's work. Carpenters carefully joined the cypress horizontal board and batten partitions and exterior framing to the limestone walls.

In 1964, former Taliesin apprentice John Howe designed a semi-detached addition with two bedrooms, bathroom, and utility room. The Kinneys have also carried out the landscaping plan Wright devised for their lot.

193

Getting there: The Kinney House is at the corner of North Fillmore Street and Pine Street. Take Madison Street north from the Courthouse square to Pine Street, turn west on Pine to North Fillmore.

Also of Interest

The Grant County Courthouse, on the square in the center of town, was built in 1902 after a design by Milwaukee architect Armand Koch. The beautifully maintained neoclassical building is most noted for its spectacular glass and copper dome. Inside the Maple St. entrance to the courthouse is a self-service tourist information center where you can pick up a brochure that maps out a walking tour of the Courthouse Square Historic District.

For General Travel Information

Contact the Lancaster Chamber of Commerce, Box 292, Lancaster, WI 53813-0292. Phone 608-723-7932.

La Crosse

19

Population 50,000. Location: La Crosse County in southwestern Wisconsin on the Mississippi River. Major highways serving the city are I-90, U.S. Hwys 14, 61, and 53.

La Crosse is the only community in Wisconsin where the Prairie School had tremendous influence on the architectural development of the city, despite the fact that neither Frank Lloyd Wright nor anyone who worked directly with him was ever involved in architectural design there.

Percy Dwight Bentley, the La Crosse native who brought Prairie style architecture to the city in 1910, had studied in Chicago, but had no contact with Sullivan, Wright, or any of their associates or followers. He was, though, well aware of the revolution in architecture brought on by what was often called the "Chicago School," and he developed great interest in Wright's work.

When he returned to La Crosse after his years in Chicago, Bentley began designing Prairie style homes, usually with designs derived from architects such as Wright and Walter Burley Griffin, designs he learned about through professional architectural journals. But Bentley was no mere mimic. His work always had original elements, and he became less and less dependent on the ideas of other architects as his career progressed.

Bentley hired Otto Merman, who had been trained in Minneapolis and La Crosse, as a draftsman, and later made him a partner. The designs that Bentley and Merman produced became a major influence on La Crosse area architecture, as local contractors and builders picked up the Prairie idiom and began producing houses in that style. As a result of Bentley's influence, more than a hundred Prairie style houses were built in La Crosse between 1910 and 1936.

The Prairie houses are concentrated in an eight-block-long area centered on Cass and King streets, which are parallel east-west streets running one block apart from downtown toward the bluffs at the edge of the city. Cass and King, and cross streets, particularly South 11th St., S. 14th St., S. 17th St., and S. 17th Place are rich in Prairie style homes. The area is easily negotiated on foot, by bicycle, or by car.

The Edward Bartl House

238 S. 17th St.
(corner of S. 17th and Cass)

Percy Bentley 1910

Private home. Not open to the public.

Brewer Edward Bartl may have been Bentley's first client. For him, Bentley designed a variation on Frank Lloyd Wright's 1907 "Fireproof House for $5000." Bentley combined elements of Wright's house, added features often used by Walter Burley Griffin, who was known for his corner piers and wraparound corner windows, added his own original ideas, and produced a charming and very livable home. Though some ideas were copied, Bentley showed great ability to synthesize different designs, add his own touches, and produce a building that doesn't feel thrown together from different sources. It feels whole and original.

The square, two-story, lap board and plaster house has a large central chimney rising from the low hipped roof. Wide eaves shelter the second story windows that wrap around the four corners. The projecting front porch was originally open, but subsequent owners added screens and storm windows.

The most interesting feature of the house is Bentley's original treatment of the stairway to the second floor. The tower, set at a 45 degree angle to the house, has tall, narrow windows that light not only the upstairs hall, but much of the living room. The Bartl house interior features a central Roman brick fireplace with an arched opening, around which are the L-shaped living-dining room, and the kitchen and pantry. The second floor contains four bedrooms, one of which opens on a sleeping porch.

Bentley created geometric-design leaded glass windows for both exterior windows and interior glass doors on built-in furniture. Woodwork and moldings, including the ceiling beams in the living-dining room, have been painted over. The fireplace, originally dark brick, was also painted tan, in an apparent attempt to lighten a rather dark interior.

Bartl owned the house for more than twenty years, after which it passed through a series of owners, some of whom made some questionable changes (like painting the fireplace). The current owners are slowly restoring the house to its original condition.

Getting there: Take Cass Street east from downtown to 17th Street.

The Henry Salzer House

1634 King St.
(corner King St. and S. 17th St.)

Percy Bentley 1912
(with assistance of Otto Merman)

Private home. Not open to the public.

Just one block away from the Bartl house is one of Bentley's most interesting commissions. Local seed merchant Henry Salzer had seen pictures of Frank Lloyd Wright houses and wanted a modern home of that type. Mrs. Salzer, though, wanted a colonial. The compromise was a modern exterior and a traditional interior. Bentley's ability to meld ideas and forms produced a home that works surprisingly well.

The exterior of the house, with its row of second-story windows, and its corner and entrance-flanking piers, is based on a Walter Burley Griffin design from 1906. Bentley was able to achieve a strong Prairie feel with the windows, the low hipped roof, and the use of horizontal elements such as a second-story string course. At the same time, his placement of the rather small fireplace on an end wall is a concession to the colonial floor plan.

The fireproof construction is of hollow tile for walls and floors, with the exterior faced with plaster.

Inside, the Salzer house is indeed traditional. The central front door opens onto an entry hall. On one side of the hall is the large living room, and adjoining living porch. On the other side are the dining room, kitchen, dining porch and den. A broad stairway leads from the hall up to the seven bedrooms. (The house as designed designated four bedrooms, a maid's room, a sewing room and a sleeping porch on the second floor.)

Though Bentley had to design a traditional floor plan, and was unable to add Prairie touches such as wood moldings on the walls, he did convince Mrs. Salzer to hire George Niedecken, who was famous as Wright's furniture builder and a proponent of Arts and Crafts and Prairie style interiors, to design the interior furnishings, rugs and curtains. A series of owners have long since dispersed the original furnishings. The interior floor plan of the home is intact, except that the kitchen has been remodeled and the porches have been enclosed.

The house, which cost Salzer $80,000, was originally a deep cream color, with brown trim and string course, and cypress roof shingles stained moss green.

Getting there: Take King Street east from downtown to South 17th Street.

Also of Interest

This block of South 17th Street and South 17th Place, one block east, contains the highest concentration of Prairie style buildings in La Crosse. In addition to the Bartl and Salzer houses, notable buildings include: The 1920 Merman-designed homes at 217 and 223 S. 17th St., adjoining houses for a contractor who had built many of the Prairie style designs of Bentley and Merman; the Ben Ott house, a stunning two-story stucco home at 241 S. 17th St., designed in 1921 by Otto Merman; the home at 229 S. 17th St., a particularly good example of a local contractor's adoption of Prairie design; the home at 232 S. 17th Place, which is a 1922 Merman design. All the remaining Prairie style homes in the 200 block of South 17th Place are examples of local contractors' work with the Prairie style.

199

The Emil Mueller House

128 S. 14th St.

Percy Bentley 1914

Private home. Not open to the public.

For brewer Mueller, Bentley designed a house inspired by Wright's 1904 plan for the Oak Park residence of Mrs. Thomas Gale, a home that is famous today for its jutting front porch and cantilevered second floor balcony. Bentley, while following much of the Gale house floor plan and creating a home that is essentially the same shape as the Gale house, used a more traditional front porch and left off the second floor balcony.

The Mueller house, which cost the brewer $45,000, sits on a long, narrow lot that is slightly higher than street level. The main entrance is on the left side, into a hall that leads to the den, which projects from the house at one side, or into the living room. Bentley liked to create long, open vistas in his designs, and in the Mueller house the front porch (originally open, now enclosed and weatherized), the living room, the dining room, and a rear dining porch (also now weatherized) run the length of the house, creating an unobstructed view from front to rear. The kitchen and former maid's room are to the side of the dining room and dining porch at the rear of the house. Clearly copied from the Gale house is the lowered living room, which is two steps below the dining room. Upstairs, the home had four bedrooms all opening on a long hallway.

The house has been altered considerably by a series of owners. Originally stucco with wood trim, in the 1960s the exterior was changed. There is now stone facing on the exterior and on the fireplace in the living room (which was originally Roman brick). The retaining wall facing the street was also faced with stone. In addition to enclosing the porches, owners removed much of the oak paneling and woodwork in the living and dining rooms (apparently in an attempt to brighten the rooms), and changed the layout of bedrooms (although there are still four). For all the changes, the essential Prairie characteristics— the low hipped roof, the rows of windows, the hidden front entrance, the massive central fireplace, and much of the original interior woodwork—is still intact.

Note the decorative pendants under the eaves at the corners of the Mueller house. The pendants, which served as downspouts for the gutters, are uniquely Bentley.

Getting there: Take King Street east from downtown to 14th Street. The Mueller house is in the first block north of King Street.

Also of Interest

Just around the corner from the Mueller house, at 1408 King St., is the C. J. Felber house, designed by Bentley in 1913. The original design focused on a formal garden (now gone) in the large back yard. The most striking feature of the house was the open stair landing, which provided a view through a sun room out into the garden. The flat-roofed garage is not original.

The Chase and Wohluter Bungalows
221 and 223 S. 11th St.

Percy Bentley 1912-1913

Private homes. Not open to the public.

These adjoining long, narrow, one-story, two-bedroom bungalows with nearly identical floor plans were built for dentist Dr. H.H. Chase and his friend Henry Wohluter. The most striking feature of each home is the polygonal living porch at the front, and the low hipped roof with very wide eaves at the corners that give the homes a solid, sheltering feel. In both houses, the exterior is lap board below the window sills and stucco above. Bentley created the geometric design for the rows of leaded glass windows in each house. The main entrance to each building is from the side, via the shared driveway. Bentley also designed matching garages for each house.

The interiors of the two houses are similar—a living porch opening onto the living room, with a dining room and the hall to the bedrooms coming off the living room. The bedrooms open onto an L-shaped hall that also provides a second access (the other is through the dining room) to the kitchen. Both homes have a rear porch facing the backyard.

202

Bentley showed considerable skill in these designs in producing homes that, although compact, have an open feel, with long vistas down the halls and through the dining room, living room, and living porch. Though the floor plans are virtually identical, Bentley's treatment of the interior—the location of the fireplace, the placement of doors, changing ceiling heights in different rooms, use of molding and other decorative woodwork, and location of built-in cabinets and sideboards are handled differently in each house, giving each a distinct feel.

Getting there: Take Cass Street east from downtown to 11th Street, then go north on 11th Street.

Also of Interest

Just a few blocks away, around the corner on Cass Street, are two fine examples of Otto Merman's work. The Dan McMillan house, 1222 Cass St., was designed by Merman in 1914, and the neighboring Gelatt house, at 1212 Cass St., is a Merman design from 1918.

More than 40 historic buildings can be seen on the Heritage Tour of the central city area. A free brochure detailing the route, for walking or driving, is available at the Swarthout Museum, 9th and Main streets, phone 608-782-1980. Museum open Tues.-Fri. 10-5, Sat.-Sun. 1-5; open Memorial Day through Labor Day Tues.-Fri. 11-5, Sat. 1-5. The Heritage Tour brochure is also available at the Visitor Center in Riverside Park downtown on the Mississippi River at the foot of State Street.

For General Travel Information

Contact the La Crosse Convention & Visitors Bureau, Riverside Park, Box 1895, La Crosse, WI 54602-1895. Phone 608-782-2366, or 800-658-9424.

Population 1,000. Location: Buffalo County in west central Wisconsin, on the Mississippi River. Access on Wis. Hwy 35. Fountain City is about 40 miles north of La Crosse.

The Martin Fugina House
348 Main St.

Percy Dwight Bentley 1916

Private home. Not open to the public.

Martin Fugina, lawyer, district attorney, and judge, was a leading citizen of Buffalo County. He was also a bank officer and a member of the local school board. His wife was active in civic organizations.

Mr. Fugina was also a man of progressive ideas. He saw Percy Bentley's homes in nearby La Crosse, and decided that Bentley was the right architect to design the new Fugina home.

Bentley created a striking Prairie style house on a hill overlooking the Mississippi River, on the main street of this small community.

The two-story, three-bedroom brick, wood, and stucco house has a living-dining room that runs the length of the first floor. A polygonal sun porch projects from the living room toward the street. A massive Roman brick fireplace dominates the living room. The house still has the original leaded glass windows, the honey-colored oak woodwork, and geometric-design pendants hanging from the corners of the soffits. The pendants, which serve as drain spouts, are a Bentley trademark.

The house has been in the Fugina family since 1916, and has been lovingly cared for. In addition to modernizing the kitchen, the family added a garage to the rear of the house. Bentley designed a garage that was not built in 1916, so the original plans were used as a guide for the new structure.

Getting there: The house is three blocks south of downtown on Main Street, which is also Wis. Hwy 35.

Also of Interest

Two blocks from the Fugina house, at 222 Main St., is a two-story stucco and wood Prairie style home. The exterior is pure Prairie School—hipped roof, overhanging eaves, bands of windows with geometric-design leaded glass, main entrance to one side —but the interior combines traditional and Prairie design elements. The central entrance hall with living and dining rooms on either side is a traditional floor plan. The beautiful green-glazed brick fireplace flanked by built-in bookcases is pure Prairie. The house is the work of a Mr. Schwartz, the contractor who built the Fugina house. A Mr. Kirschner, a local man who worked on the river, liked the Fugina house but couldn't afford an architect. He asked Schwartz to essay a Prairie house without benefit of architect. Schwartz complied. Fugina was furious.

Six miles south of Fountain City and across the Mississippi is Winona, Minnesota, the site of four beautiful works by George Maher, and Purcell and Elmslie. Maher's designs are the Winona Savings Bank, at 204 Main St., and the J.R. Watkins Company administration building, at 150 Liberty St. The Purcell and Elmslie buildings are the Merchants Bank, at Third and Lafayette, one of their masterpieces, and the J.W.S. Gallagher house, at 451 West Broadway. The two banks and the J.R. Watkins Company welcome visitors during regular business hours. Stop at the public library, 151 W. Fifth St., or at the Convention and Visitors Bureau, 67 Main St., for a map and historic walking tour information.

For General Travel Information

Contact the Buffalo County Clerk, Courthouse Annex, Alma, WI 54610. Phone 608-685-4940.

Tomah

Population 7,700. Location: Monroe County in west central Wisconsin. Access is on I-90/94 and U.S. Hwy 12.

Tomah Public Library
716 Superior Ave.
Tomah, WI 54660

Claude and Starck 1916

Open Memorial Day-Labor Day: Monday, Wednesday, Friday 10-5; Tuesday, Thursday 10-8; Saturday noon-4. Rest of the year: Monday-Thursday 10-8, Friday-Saturday 10-5. Phone 608-372-4569.

Detail of the frieze

In 1871 Tomah city leaders began a hundred-volume library assembled through donations of books and magazines by local residents. The Ladies Library Association soon took over the operation, but as the collection outgrew several successive locations the city took over again because volunteer operation was no longer adequate.

In 1911 Ernest Buckley, who was a successful geologist, left the city $12,000 in his will to be used as needed for a park and/or a library. City leaders set aside $7000 of Buckley's bequest for a library, and requested a grant of $10,000 from the Carnegie Foundation. By 1915 they had received the Carnegie grant and had secured the services of Claude and Starck, who were well known in the Midwest for their library designs for small communities.

The architects produced the last of the four Wisconsin versions of their "Sullivanesque" design—a two-story (raised basement and main floor), red brick rectangle topped by a green-tiled hipped roof with overhanging eaves. A buff-color abstract floral design frieze surmounts the walls at the base of the soffit. (The frieze is made of staff, a molded gypsum and fiber material that was manufactured by the American Decorating Company of Chicago.) Rows of windows set within the frieze provided light from all directions while allowing plenty of wall space for bookshelves. Large windows flanking the entrance vestibule provided additional light to the reading areas on the main floor. The interior represented Claude and Starck's standard, and very functional, library design. The entry led visitors to a mid-level between the basement, which housed community rooms and a classroom, and the main floor, where the library stacks were. The library included a fireplace, built-in bookshelves and magazine racks along the walls, built-in benches, and a desk on the rear wall facing the main entrance (from where the librarian could easily keep watch over the entire room).

The Tomah library eventually outgrew the Claude and Starck building, and in 1980 an addition, designed by the Madison firm of Potter, Lawson and Pawlowsky, was completed. The flat-roofed, red-brick addition connects to the rear of the original library, allowing Claude and Starck's graceful design to remain the center of attention.

While much of the original woodwork and built-in furniture has been lost in the process of modernization, the original leaded glass windows remain. A portion of the frieze, removed during the 1980 remodeling, is on view in the basement of the library addition.

Getting there: U.S. Hwy 12 becomes Superior Avenue in downtown Tomah.

Also of Interest

Tomah resident Alois Fix saw the Percy Bentley-designed Bartl house in La Crosse (see p. 196) and immediately wanted one like it. Bentley obliged in 1912 with a striking Prairie home at 1403 Kilbourn Ave. The Fix house is an upscale version of the Bartl house; Bentley used brick instead of wood for the corner piers and front porch. The house is at the corner of Kilbourn and East Holton. Kilbourn is one block east of, and runs parallel to, Superior Avenue.

For General Travel Information

Contact the Tomah Chamber of Commerce, Box 625, Tomah, WI 54660-0625. Phone 608-372-2166, or 800-368-3601.

209

22 Eau Claire

Population 56,000. Location: Eau Claire County in west central Wisconsin. Major access roads are I-94 from west and south, and U.S. Hwy 53 from north and south.

First Congregational Church Community House

310 Broadway
Eau Claire, WI 54702

Purcell and Elmslie 1914

Open 8:30-4 Monday-Friday. Phone 715-834-2668.

Along with the settlers and lumberjacks, missionaries and ministers also arrived in northern Wisconsin in the mid-19th century. Eau Claire's First Congregational Church was organized in 1856, and by 1858 had its own building on the site where the present church stands. The Congregational Church must have prospered, because by 1887 the wooden clapboard church had been sold and moved, and a large stone Romanesque style church, costing some $50,000, had been erected.

Cornelia Ingram, wife of lumber baron O. H. Ingram and a long-time church member, died in 1912, leaving a bequest to the church to be used for construction of a community house.

The logical place for the new structure was to the side of the church, on the spot where the parsonage stood. The parsonage was destroyed, and Mrs. Peter Truax, widow of a wealthy farmer, donated two lots a block from the church on Third Avenue as the site for the new parsonage. Purcell and Elmslie were hired to design the two new buildings.

At this time, the firm was experimenting with designs based on a steeply pitched roof with a front-facing gable. Their community house design incorporated the simple lines of the high gable along with wide eaves that shelter the low tan sandstone walls. They completed the design with rows of casement windows below, a triangular grouping of stained glass windows in both front and rear gables, and exposed roof beams, producing a striking, graceful building that blended well with the more traditional church to which it was attached.

The interior of the Community House centered on a long assembly room that ran the length of the building, with smaller rooms at each corner, and on one side a large classroom with a folding wall that could be opened to expand the size of the assembly room. A kitchen opened off the entry hall, which also connected the Community House to the church.

A disastrous fire in 1918 destroyed the church, but did only minimal damage to the Community House. Three years, and nearly $210,000 later, the present Gothic church was dedicated (there is no record as to why Purcell and Elmslie were not chosen to design the new church). The church is built of the same tan sandstone, cut in blocks of roughly the same size and shape, as those in the Community House.

Over the years, the Community House has been remodeled and altered to remove several interior walls, relocate and enlarge the kitchen, and expand the entrance hall. The stained and leaded glass windows are largely intact, as is a brick fireplace and much of the original woodwork.

Original plans called for plantings, a narrow walk and a small semicircular reflecting pool in front of the Community House. The landscape plan was not carried out.

Getting there: Take Lake Street west from downtown across the Chippewa River. Turn south on Third Avenue to Broadway, then west on Broadway to the Community House.

First Congregational Church Parsonage
403 Third Ave.

Purcell and Elmslie 1914

Private home. Not open to the public.

When Mrs. Ingram left money in her will for a new community house, the location of which required removal of the old parsonage, Purcell and Elmslie were retained to design the new parsonage as well as the community house.

Church leaders could afford only a modest residence to be built on the lots donated by Mrs. Truax a block down Third Avenue from the church, so Purcell and Elmslie produced a design based on a gardener's cottage they had built for a large estate in Woods Hole, Massachusetts.

The parsonage's steeply-pitched roof with no eaves on the front facing gable was a variation on the firm's pitched roof, front gable designs of this period. The wood and plaster parsonage, which cost $5,900, had an open floor plan designed around a central brick fireplace with two faces. One fireplace faced into the living room, and the one on the opposite side faced into the pastor's den. The kitchen and a dining room with doors opening to a side porch completed the downstairs plan. Upstairs, there were three bedrooms.

In 1941, the church expanded the parsonage with the addition of the front section of the house, which is offset to the right of the original home. This remodeling enlarged the living room and added a fourth bedroom upstairs.

The church sold the parsonage in 1978, and the two subsequent owners have carefully restored and maintained both interior and exterior. The exterior is painted to copy the 1914 paint scheme in reverse: Originally the house was dark and the trim was light, whereas today the house is painted cream with dark brown decorative trim.

Getting there: Take Lake Street west from downtown across the Chippewa River to Third Avenue. Turn south and go three blocks to the parsonage.

The J.D.R. Steven House

606 Second Ave. (sometimes listed as 216 Hudson Ave.)

Purcell and Feick 1909

Private home. Not open to the public.

J.D.R. Steven came to Eau Claire from New Brunswick, Canada, in 1901, when he was 17. He initially worked in the lumber industry, becoming a partner in the Steven & Jarvis Lumbering Company in 1907. However, he is better known in city history for his later position as principal owner and president of the Eau Claire Book & Stationery Company, and for his work with fraternal and charitable organizations in the city. By 1909, the 28-year-old Steven was married, with children. He and his wife retained Purcell and Feick to build them a suitable home.

Architectural historians consider the Steven house a benchmark in Purcell and Feick's development of open plan homes. Their cruciform plan, which incorporated a central fireplace around which other rooms are arranged, was used throughout the remainder of their careers (and that of Elmslie, after he joined the firm later in 1909). The plan was also adopted by many other architects.

The Steven house was built into a hill, the slope of which was leveled considerably with fill. The house is placed well back on the lot, with the main entrance next to the porch (on the right as viewed from Second Avenue). The first floor of the wood-and-stucco home contains a kitchen and sewing room to the rear, the dining room to the left side as viewed from Second Avenue, and the living room, which thrusts forward toward Second Avenue.

A massive brick fireplace faced with Portuguese ceramic tile of dark red-green tones dominates the living room and separates it from the other rooms. Placement of the fireplace was so important to the design that the flue was routed around upstairs doorways rather than moving the fireplace so the flue could be straight.

Upstairs are four bedrooms, each with its own sink, and a full bathroom. (A sink in the bedroom was considered the height of luxury at a time when most people didn't have indoor plumbing at all.) The master bedroom takes up the entire second story facade that faces Second Avenue—a large bedroom for that time. The house is built into the hill, so the side facing Second Ave. had a finished playroom for the Steven children with windows at ground level.

The Steven House is essentially intact. Furniture and light fixtures were removed or lost, and an unobtrusive garage was added on the Hudson Street side. The kitchen entrance was remodeled and the kitchen porch was enclosed to create a breakfast nook. The changes did not alter the basic floor plan or change the character of the home. The beautiful wood moldings above the windows and on the ceiling of the living and dining rooms are completely intact, and exterior colors are the same as the original.

Behind the Steven house, at 218 Hudson St., is the Steven Cottage, designed by Purcell and Feick at the same time they completed the larger house. The cottage was built for Mrs. Steven's mother, and its main entrance is at the side, just a few steps away from the kitchen entrance to the Steven House. The cottage has been heavily remodeled, and aluminum siding has replaced the original shingle siding. However, the original roofline is intact.

Getting there: Take Lake Street west from downtown across the Chippewa River to Second Avenue. Turn south on Second Avenue.

215

Also of Interest

As a 19th and early 20th-century center for lumbering and manufacturing, Eau Claire has many fine historic buildings. The Eau Claire Landmarks Commission has a book listing all the city and National Register landmarks, with maps and a description of each building. A walking tour of the three areas described in the book is well worth the time of anyone with an interest in historic buildings. The book costs $3.00 and can be obtained from the Landmarks Commission, City Hall, 203 South Farwell St., Eau Claire, WI 54701; phone 715-839-4947.

Like most architectural firms, Purcell, Feick and Elmslie designed in a variety of styles. In 1910, the firm produced the parish house for the Christ Church Cathedral in Tudor Revival style, and in 1916 Purcell and Elmslie produced a new Christ Church Cathedral in Gothic Revival style. They are in the 500 block of South Farwell Street, in downtown Eau Claire. Both are detailed in the Landmarks Commission book.

For General Travel Information

Contact the Eau Claire Area Convention & Visitors Bureau, 2127 Brackett Ave., Eau Claire, WI 54701. Phone 715-839-2919, or 800-344-FUNN.

Barron

Population 3,000. Location: Barron County in northwest Wisconsin. Access is on U.S. Hwy 53, then west on U.S. Hwy 8. Barron is about 45 miles north of Eau Claire.

Barron Public Library
10 North Third St.
Barron, WI 54812

Claude and Starck 1913

Open Monday, Wednesday, Thursday 10-7:30, Tuesday 10-6, Friday 10-5, Saturday 9-noon. Phone 715-537-3881.

As the northwoods community of Barron grew after the turn of the century, the Men's Club, an organization of leading business and professional leaders, took on the

Barron Public Library frieze detail

task of organizing a library. They solicited books and other materials through door-to-door canvassing, and opened the library in a room above the post office in April, 1909. The library grew as donations increased, and the librarian was eventually given funds to buy books and periodicals. By early 1912 it had outgrown a second location, and city leaders decided to build a larger, permanent facility.

They received a $6,500 grant from the Carnegie Foundation, purchased a lot for $500, and hired the firm of Claude and Starck to design a modest library building.

By 1912 Claude and Starck had firmly established themselves as prominent designers of libraries and schools. Since 1903, they had designed libraries for Baraboo, Delavan, Columbus, Ladysmith, and a number of other small communities in Wisconsin, Minnesota, and Illinois. Though the firm designed in classical style, they had begun as early as 1908 (see Evansville, p. 141) to design libraries in what was called "modern" or "Sullivanesque" style, and they chose this approach for the Barron building.

The library that opened in February, 1913, is a two-story red brick building with a main floor resting on a raised basement. The entry vestibule leads visitors to a mid-level between the basement, which originally housed a large community room, and the main floor, which contained the library stacks. The hipped, red-tile roof extends protectively outward, its wide eaves sheltering an abstract floral design frieze along the upper walls. (The catalog-order frieze is of staff, a molded gypsum/fiber material.) Windows in the frieze, as well as larger double windows flanking the entrance vestibule, provide light and ventilation. Even on a limited budget, the firm was able to provide an elegant leaded-glass design in the front upper windows and in the glass panels adjoining the main entrance.

The library has been well maintained, and original woodwork, windows and librarian's desk are intact. Today, the library is filled to overflowing, and the city plans to build an addition onto the building.

Getting there: Hwy 8 becomes East Division Street in Barron. The library is on the corner of East Division and North Third Street.

For General Travel Information

Contact the Barron County Clerk, Courthouse, Barron, WI 54812. Phone 715-537-6200.

24   Spooner

Population 2,800. Location: Washburn County in northwest Wisconsin. Access is on U.S. Hwy 53, U.S. Hwy 63, and Wis. Hwy 70. Spooner is 80 miles north of Eau Claire.

Mrs. Richard Polson House
Rustic Road

Purcell and Elmslie 1917

Private home. Not open to the public.

Mrs. Polson was a wealthy Chicago woman who commissioned Purcell and Elmslie to build this modest home as a wedding present for her son, D. B. Brockett, and

Polson house front entrance

his wife Nan. Local lore has it that Nan was a divorcee, and to escape scandal the couple lived in northern Wisconsin.

Mr. Brockett worked on the railroad and raised dairy cattle. The couple had owned the house for only a few years when Mr. Brockett was killed by a train while trying to cross the tracks just west of his home to take milk to the dairy. Supposedly, his wife, coming home from a prayer meeting, was on the train that killed her husband.

Mrs. Brockett left town, selling the house to a local family, who lived in it for many years but did little to maintain it. The current owner has put considerable effort into restoration.

The home Mrs. Polson commissioned is an example of Purcell and Elmslie's small and inexpensive open-plan houses. (It is estimated that the house cost about $3000 to build.) The firm built a number of similar homes for clients in Minnesota. The most interesting exterior design features on this wood-and-stucco home are the asymmetrical gabled roof and the rows of narrow casement windows on both the first and second floors.

The high gable and steeply pitched roof became almost a design trademark of Purcell and Elmslie. (Though used by Frank Lloyd Wright for his home in Oak Park, it was not used consistently by any other Prairie School architects except Purcell and Elmslie. For variations on the theme, see the First Congregational Church Community House and Parsonage in Eau Claire, pp. 210 and 212.)

The first floor interior of the house was designed around a central red brick fireplace, with the living room in front, and the dining room, kitchen, and bedroom to the rear of the fireplace mass. A sun porch off the living room and a porch off the kitchen completed the first floor. The second floor was originally left unfinished. Local lore has it that the Brocketts intended to make the second floor into a nursery, but had no children at the time Mr. Brockett was killed. The current owner has divided the upstairs into bedrooms and a bathroom.

The current owner also restored the original trellised front entrance and enlarged the rear bedroom by enclosing the kitchen porch.

Getting there: The Polson House is on Rustic Road, just north of downtown off U.S. Hwy 63. Turn east on Front Street, then immediately on to Rustic Road, crossing the railroad tracks where Mr. Brockett was killed.

For General Travel Information

Contact the Spooner Chamber of Commerce, Box 406, Spooner, WI 54801-0406. Phone 715-635-2168.

Stevens Point

25

Population 23,000. Location: Portage County in central Wisconsin, access on U.S. Hwy 51 and U.S. Hwy 10.

The Frank Iber House
Springville Dr. at Business Hwy 51

Frank Lloyd Wright 1956

Private home. Not open to the public.

The Iber house is a four-bedroom version of the first Erdman prefab home (see p. 128). The house has a full basement and a garage and is partially faced with stone rather than the standard Masonite.

Getting there: Take Business Hwy 51 south from Stevens Point. Springville Dr. meets the highway just south of the Little Plover River between the villages of Whiting and Plover. Turn west.

Also of Interest

Stevens Point has an interesting downtown historic district. Pick up the brochure "Gateway to the Pineries," which contains a walking tour and other information, at the library, City Hall, or Chamber of Commerce.

For General Travel Information

Contact the Chamber of Commerce, 600 Main St., Stevens Point, WI 54481. Phone 715-344-2556, or 800-236-INFO.

Wausau

26

Population 34,000. Location: Marathon County in north central Wisconsin. Access on U.S. Hwy 51, and Wis. Hwy 29.

The Hiram Stewart House
521 Grant St.
Wausau, WI 54401

George Maher 1905

Operated year-round as the Stewart Inn by Joy Horsch. Tours also available. Phone 715-848-2864. Please call in advance if you want to tour the house.

Lumberman Hiram Stewart moved to Wausau from Michigan in the mid-1880s. He and a partner operated the Barker & Stewart Lumber Company.

By the early years of the 20th century, Stewart had made his fortune, and he commissioned George Maher to design for him a house befitting his civic and business prominence. How Stewart came to choose Maher is not known, but several other Wausau business leaders had Maher-designed homes, and Maher was also designing the Wausau Public Library (now remodeled so as to eliminate virtually all traces of Maher), when Stewart began his search for an architect.

Stewart was a rich beneficiary of Maher's creative genius. The massive blue-gray stucco house is one of the best examples of Maher's version of Prairie School design. The Stewart House gives a nod to standard Prairie style in its narrow bands of horizontal exterior molding, in its hipped roof, and the use of stucco as the main building material.

By the time he designed the Stewart house, Maher had perfected his "motif-rhythm" theory. This approach to design used a local plant and/or a geometric shape as the unifying theme throughout the house. For Stewart, Maher chose the tulip and the three-segment (tripartite) arch, elements which are ubiquitous throughout the house. On the exterior, the entrance doors are arched, and tulips crown the columns on the front porch.

The interior of the Stewart House is spectacular. The eighteen rooms include five bedrooms on the second floor and a third-floor ball room, and contain six fireplaces. A dozen kinds of wood were used in the paneling, moldings, stair railings, cabinets, and built-in benches, buffet, and bookshelves. The tulip is seen in the light fixtures and leaded-glass windows. The tripartite arch is everywhere—in the shape of windows, in door frames, the top of a bookcase, the fireplace screen, even in a garage window.

The sweeping beamed-ceiling living room, dominated by a massive brick fireplace framed by a dazzling glass mosaic, is the most spectacular living space in Wausau.

In 1913 the Stewart family sold their house and moved to California. The second owner's family sold it in 1964, after which it went through a series of owners who let it deteriorate.

The Horsches bought it in 1988 and spent a year restoring the home to its original glory. It is a must on any architectural tour of Wausau.

Getting there: From downtown Wausau, go north on any numbered street (First-Sixth) to Grant Street.

The A.P. Woodson House
410 McIndoe St.

George Maher 1914

Now owned by Immanuel Baptist Church. Open 8-11:30 and 1-5 Monday-Friday. Visitors are asked to stop at the church office upon arrival. Phone 715-842-1240.

In 1911, lumberman and local business leader Cyrus Yawkey commissioned George Maher to remodel his classical revival home at 403 McIndoe St. Maher accordingly remodeled the interior into his version of a Prairie style home.

Also in 1911, Leigh, Cyrus' only child, married Kansas businessman Aytchemonde P. Woodson. She wanted to stay in Wausau near her friends and relatives, so Cyrus offered his son-in-law a job. George Maher was retained to build a house for the Woodsons on a lot across the street from the home of Leigh's parents.

The brick mansion Maher produced is a surprisingly pleasing Prairie-meets-Tudor concoction. It includes both Prairie elements—the rows of windows, the hipped roof—along with a Tudor revival chimney. Maher was, at this point in his career,

227

beginning to design in classical revival styles, and would eventually cease to design Prairie style buildings.

Maher used his "motif-rhythm" approach to design, in the Woodson house incorporating the lotus plant, a foliage arrangement, and the arch as the unifying design elements. They appear in the main entrance and throughout the house in leaded glass windows, woodwork, door and window frames, ceiling designs, and (originally) in Maher-designed furniture and light fixtures.

The Woodsons owned the house until 1954, when they moved to another Wausau home. The Immanuel Baptist Church eventually purchased the house, and now uses it for classrooms, offices, and a library. A number of leaded and stained glass windows have been removed from the house, as has much of the Maher-designed furniture. However, the room arrangement is basically intact, and much of the woodwork and some of the built-in furniture is still in the house. An attached bell tower and a rear addition distract from the integrity of the house.

Getting there: From downtown Wausau, take 1st, 3rd or 4th street north to McIndoe Street.

The Charles Manson House
1224 Highland Park Blvd.

Frank Lloyd Wright 1938

Private home. Not open to the public.

Charles and Dorothy Manson were active in Wausau business and civic affairs. He ran the family insurance agency, while she was a member of the League of Women Voters, the Wausau Civic Music Association, and other public-interest organizations. They were both well educated, well traveled, and interested in arts and culture—perfect clients for Frank Lloyd Wright. And when Charles read about the newly-built Jacobs I house in Madison (see p. 121), he immediately contacted Wright.

The Manson house was Wright's fourth completed Usonian design. The flat-roofed, red brick, plywood-and-cypress home sits on a concrete slab, in which are embedded the pipes for the radiant heating system (which no longer works). The sandwich walls are five layers thick—three layers of plywood faced on both sides with horizontal cypress board and batten—two layers thicker than in other Usonians, in recognition of Wausau's fierce winters.

229

Wright's design for the Mansons was unlike anything Wausau contractors had seen before. It took more than a year to obtain final plans and bids, all of which exceeded the Mansons' $7500 budget. The house that was completed in mid-1941 by local contractor Bill Anderes eventually cost nearly $15,000.

The house descends three levels down a sloping lot. Entry is through the carport (now largely enclosed for storage) and down three steps into a narrow, 44-foot-long hall. The three bedrooms come off this low gallery, which leads past the kitchen and down three more steps to the high-ceilinged living room with its massive brick fireplace. French doors open off the living room onto a terrace.

Though Usonians were intended for economical living, the Manson house had a maid's room. The ceilings in the children's bedrooms were dropped to accommodate the maid's room and a darkroom (Mr. Manson's hobby was photography) in a second story that rises only a few feet above the roof of the bedroom wing.

The three-level design plus the different heights of the two-story high kitchen stack and the maid's room give the Manson house a complex, multi-layered look.

Wright created some extra items for the house, including a built-in radio-phonograph unit with speaker cabinets, storage for records, and space for the equipment. He also designed a wooden clothes drying rack for the kitchen. The rack was lowered, loaded with clothes, then hoisted up out of the way using a rope attached to a pulley secured high on the kitchen wall.

The Mansons loved the house, and except for a smoking fireplace (which was corrected by adding rows of brick to decrease the size of the opening) they had no complaints. After their deaths in the 1960s, the house went through a series of owners. The current owner is restoring damage caused by previous lack of maintenance.

Getting there: From downtown Wausau, go north on 6th Street to Franklin Street. Turn right (east) on Franklin to 13th Street. Turn left (north) to Highland Park Boulevard.

230

The Granville Jones House
915 Grant St.

George Maher 1905-06

Private home. Not open to the public.

Granville Jones came to Wisconsin from New York state in 1872, when he was fifteen. He studied at the University of Wisconsin in Madison, and worked as principal of the high school in Grand Rapids (now Wisconsin Rapids). He moved to Wausau in 1884 to study law with a local firm, but eventually made his fortune in real estate. Jones is best known in Wisconsin history for his terms on the University of Wisconsin Board of Regents, where he consistently advocated (unsuccessfully) censoring what the faculty could teach and who they could invite to the University as speakers.

By the early 1900s, Jones, his wife, and four daughters comprised one of the leading Wausau families. They wanted a larger and finer home than the Queen Anne house they lived in, and Jones, who had seen Maher's work in the suburbs of Chicago,

231

retained the architect to design a mansion.

Jones moved their existing home off the large hillside lot with its sweeping view of the city and the Wisconsin River valley.

Maher, who also designed the landscaping for the lot, produced a massive stucco edifice with a hipped roof and overhanging eaves. The house was said to have Wausau's first picture window. As with his other residences for wealthy clients, Maher used many kinds of wood for paneling, moldings, door and window frames, cabinets, stair railings, and decoration throughout the house. The unifying motifs for the Jones house were the arch and the water lily. The lily was found in leaded glass windows and light fixtures, glass door panels, carved wood decorations, and in a beautiful glass mosaic set in the brick above the living room fireplace.

In the 1920s, Jones suffered financial reverses and had to sell his home. It went through a series of owners, some of whom altered the house considerably—porches were enclosed, the picture window was replaced by a bay window, many leaded glass windows were removed, as were original furnishings and fixtures, and much of the interior woodwork was removed. The house was originally a henna red. It is now a light gray. Nevertheless, it is still discernably Maher.

Getting there: Take 6th Street north from downtown to Franklin Street. Turn right (east) on Franklin to LaSalle Street. Turn right (south) on LaSalle one block to Grant Street, then left (east) on Grant.

State Historical Society of Wisconsin

The Duey Wright House
904 Grand Ave.

Frank Lloyd Wright 1957

Private home. Not open to the public.

   Music store owner Duey Wright (no relation to Frank Lloyd Wright) and his wife Julia, who owned a lot overlooking the Wisconsin River just south of downtown Wausau, hired Frank Lloyd Wright to design their home.
   Wright's first design for the couple was a dramatic structure sited parallel to the river and supported by a massive retaining wall. That plan proved to be too costly for the Wrights, who asked for something involving a little less earth moving.
   The second version, which was completed after Frank Lloyd Wright's death in 1959, turned the house 90 degrees from the original design. The concrete block structure has a large living-dining-kitchen area that is rounded on the side that faces the

233

river. A squared-cornered, slightly pitched hipped roof covers the living area. The master bedroom adjoins this living space, giving the bedroom a view of the river. A long wing containing bedrooms and ending in the carport extends back from the living room, away from the river. The roughly L-shaped house, with its rounded living area and long bedroom wing, is said to be designed on a musical note motif that is also echoed in the cutout wood panels in the clerestories and elsewhere.

The house is still in the Duey Wright family.

Due to landscaping on the large lot, the house is virtually impossible to see from the road or other public areas during the time of year when the trees are leafed out.

Getting there: The house is on Grand Avenue (Business Hwy 51) just south of downtown Wausau.

Also of Interest

George Maher designed two other homes in Wausau, the 1894 Gilbert House, a two-story shingle style at 904 Franklin St., and the colonial revival Ross House, at 604 Franklin St., built in 1920. Maher also designed the public library, which has been enlarged and remodeled so as to obliterate Maher's original design.

Wausau has a rich architectural heritage, and a day spent in the historic residential areas north and east of downtown is well worthwhile. To help you find your way, a guide to Wausau's historic architecture is available at the Wausau Historical Museum (which happens to be the Maher-remodeled Yawkey mansion). For more information, contact the Wausau Historical Museum, 403 McIndoe St. Phone 715-848-6143. The museum is open 9-4:30 Tuesday-Thursday, and 1-4:30 on Saturday and Sunday.

For General Travel Information

Contact the Wausau Area Convention & Visitors Council, Box 6190, Wausau, WI 54402-6190. Phone 715-845-6231, or 800-236-WSAU.

Merrill

27

Population 10,100. Location: Lincoln County in north central Wisconsin, twenty miles north of Wausau on U.S. Hwy 51. Take Business Hwy 51 into the city.

T.B. Scott Free Library
106 W. First St.

Claude and Starck 1911

Open Monday-Friday 9-5:30 (Thursday open until 8 p.m.), Saturday 9-noon. Phone 715-536-7191.

Detail of the frieze

T.B. Scott, pioneer lumberman, state senator, and the first mayor of Merrill, bequeathed $10,000 to the city for a library when he died in 1886. The town fathers used the money to build a new city hall, in which the library was housed for nearly 20 years. The library outgrew its allotted space almost immediately, and after about ten years of discussing different ways to solve the problem, in 1909 the city accepted a $17,500 Carnegie Foundation grant for a new library. Local lumberman A.H. Stange donated the site—an old landfill on the banks of the Prairie River just west of downtown Merrill.

The library building committee retained Claude and Starck, who had developed a reputation as designers of small libraries, to produce the new facility. The design they offered was a variation of the "Sullivanesque" or "modern" design they had produced for the Evansville library (see p. 141), and would eventually use for the Tomah (see p. 207) and Barron (see p. 217) libraries.

The Claude and Starck design is a two-story (raised basement and main floor) red brick rectangle with a small projection at the rear. A buff-color abstract floral design frieze surmounts the walls beneath the eaves. (The frieze is of staff, a molded gypsum/fiber material that was manufactured on special order by the American Decorating Company of Chicago.) Windows are placed in a row along the walls within the frieze. Additional large triplet windows flank the entrance vestibule. A low, hipped, red-tile roof tops the building. The entrance vestibule deposits patrons on a mid-level between the first floor and basement, which contained a community room for local meetings and other uses.

The librarian's office, with wood and glass partitions and a circulation desk facing the main entrance allowed the librarian to see the entire floor. The interior included built-in bookshelves along the walls and a dark brown brick fireplace. The original interior is remarkably intact.

In 1969, the library needed more space, and the Wausau firm of Shavie and Murray designed a low, unobtrusive red brick addition that connects to the rear of the original library, allowing Claude and Starck's graceful and dignified building to maintain its role as center of attention. The original building is now used as the children's library.

Getting there: Take Business Hwy 51 into downtown Merrill. Turn west on Wis. Hwy 64 and go about a mile to the library.

Also of Interest

The old American State Bank, a Prairie-style rectangular block designed in 1924 by Chicago architect A.H. Hubbard, is now used by a telephone company as a switching station. All but two of the stained glass windows have been bricked up, but the beautiful terra cotta trim and entrance ornamentation is still intact. At 1000 W. Main St., three blocks west of Business 51.

The 1902 Lincoln County Courthouse is an exuberant melange of classical styles. A wonderful and well-maintained reminder of everything Frank Lloyd Wright and the Prairie School architects were rebelling against. At the corner of Business 51 and West Main St. in downtown Merrill. Open weekdays during office hours, and some evenings and weekends when public meetings are held.

For General Travel Information

Contact the Merrill Chamber of Commerce, 201 N. Center Ave., Merrill, WI 54452. Phone 715-476-2389.

28

Rhinelander

Population 8,000. Location: Oneida County in north central Wisconsin. Rhinelander is 60 miles north of Wausau. Take U.S. Hwy 51 north to Merrill, then Wis. Hwy 17 to Rhinelander. U.S. Hwy 8 provides east-west access to Rhinelander.

State Historical Society of Wisconsin

First National Bank soon after opening

First National Bank
8 W. Davenport St.

Purcell and Elmslie 1910-1911

Building now occupied by Valley Bank. Open 9-4:30 Monday-Thursday, 9-6 Friday. Phone 715-362-6900.

Terra cotta ornament designed by George Elmslie

By 1910, Rhinelander was a prosperous northwoods city, a center of government, commerce and manufacturing. The Bank of Rhinelander, founded in 1888, had grown to become the First National Bank of Rhinelander, and Dr. Alfred Daniels, a physician, businessman and president of the bank, wanted to hire a progressive architectural firm to design a new building for the institution.

Purcell and Elmslie had been in partnership for only a year, but had already designed a bank for Grand Meadow, Minnesota. The Rhinelander bank was the firm's second, and their only Wisconsin bank.

The firm produced a two-story red brick and white sandstone rectangle. The building feels low and horizontal, an effect created by the flat roof, plain stone cornice, and row of second floor windows. The heavy sandstone surrounding the entrances gives a solid, secure feel to the building, an important attribute for a bank. The second floor contained rental offices in an L shape around a skylight. The main floor housed both the bank, in the rear, and shops, with their windows facing Davenport St.

239

Elmslie designed intricate terra cotta ornament for the exterior walls and for the facade above the main entrance. Weathering has obscured much of the original color, but green and other subtle shades can still be seen.

The building interior has been totally remodeled. The entire first floor is now occupied by a bank. The second floor skylight was removed to provide for more office space, and an unobtrusive addition was attached to the rear. Only the arched entry way remains from the original interior.

However, with the exception of an added bank sign and the closing off of two secondary entrances, the exterior remains much as Purcell and Elmslie designed it.

Getting there: Davenport Street crosses Wis. Hwy 17 in the center of downtown Rhinelander.

Also of Interest

The Oneida County Courthouse, a 1908 neo-classical pile of limestone, is beautifully maintained and has a spectacular stained glass dome. It's just two blocks down Davenport Street from the bank.

For General Travel Information

Contact the Rhinelander Chamber of Commerce, 135 S. Stevens St., City Hall, Rhinelander, WI 54501. Phone 715-362-7464.

Buildings Open to the Public

For specific information, see the listing for each building

Baraboo	Baraboo High School (now the Civic Center)
Barron	Barron Public Library
Columbus	Columbus Public Library Farmers and Merchants Union Bank
Eau Claire	First Congregational Church Community House
Evansville	Eager Free Public Library
Jefferson	Jefferson Public Library (now Carnegie Building)
Lancaster	Municipal Building and Grantland Theater
Madison	Bradley House I Collins House Spring Trail Stonework Unitarian Meeting House
Merrill	T.B. Scott Public Library
Milwaukee	Annunciation Greek Orthodox Church
Racine	Johnson Wax Administration Building Wingspread

Reedsburg	Reedsburg Public Library
Rhinelander	First National Bank (now Valley Bank)
Richland Center	A.D. German Warehouse
Spring Green	Spring Green Restaurant Taliesin Complex
Tomah	Tomah Public Library
Wausau	Stewart House (now Stewart Inn) Woodson House (now Immanuel Baptist Church)
Wisconsin Dells	Kilbourn Public Library Seth Peterson Cottage Sherman House

Chronological Listing of Buildings by Architect

The date is the year the building was designed. Occasionally, construction occurred some years later. See the individual building listings for details.

Frank Lloyd Wright

Romeo and Juliet Tower: 1896, Spring Green
Wallis-Goldsmith House: 1900, Delavan
Hillside School: 1902, Spring Green
Spencer House: 1902, Delavan
Ross House: 1902, Delavan
Jones Estate and Gatehouse: 1903, Delavan
Robert Lamp House: 1903, Madison
A.P. Johnson House: 1905, Delavan
Thomas Hardy House: 1905, Racine
Porter House (Tan-y-deri): 1907, Spring Green
Eugene Gilmore House: 1908, Madison
Taliesin I: 1911, Spring Green
Taliesin II: 1914, Spring Green
A.D. German Warehouse: 1915, Richland Center
Frederick Bogk House: 1916, Milwaukee
American System Built Homes: 1911-16, Milwaukee
Stephen Hunt House: 1917, Oshkosh
Taliesin III: 1925, Spring Green
Spring Trail Stonework (attributed): 1926, Madison
Herbert Jacobs House I: 1936, Madison
Johnson Wax Administration Building: 1936, Racine
Herbert Johnson House, "Wingspread": 1937, Racine
Midway Farm (Taliesin complex): 1938 & 1947, Spring Green
Charles Manson House: 1938, Wausau
Bernard Schwartz House: 1939, Two Rivers
John Pew House: 1939, Madison
Herbert Jacobs House II: 1944, Middleton
Johnson Wax Research Tower: 1944, Racine
Unitarian Meeting House: 1947, Madison
Albert Adelman House: 1948, Fox Point

Richard Smith House: 1950, Jefferson
Patrick Kinney House: 1951, Lancaster
Willard Keland House: 1954, Racine
Maurice Greenberg House: 1954, Dousman
Clarke Arnold House: 1954, Columbus
Annunciation Greek Orthodox Church: 1956, Milwaukee
Wyoming Valley School: 1956, Spring Green
Marshall Erdman Prefab # 1: 1956
      Van Tamelen House, Madison
      Jackson House, Beaver Dam
      Iber House, Stevens Point
      Mollica House, Bayside
Marshall Erdman Prefab # 2: 1957
      Rudin House, Madison
Duey Wright House: 1957, Wausau
Seth Peterson Cottage: 1958, Lake Delton

Louis Sullivan

Bradley House I: 1909, Madison
Farmers & Merchants Union Bank: 1919, Columbus

Purcell and Feick

J.D.R. Steven House: 1909, Eau Claire

Purcell and Elmslie

First National Bank: 1910-11, Rhinelander
First Congregational Church Community House: 1914, Eau Claire
First Congregational Church Parsonage: 1914, Eau Claire
Bradley House II: 1914-15, Madison
Mrs. Richard Polson House: 1917, Spooner

George Maher

Hiram Stewart House: 1905, Wausau
Granville Jones House: 1905-06, Wausau

Edward Elliott House: 1910, Madison
A.P. Woodson House: 1914, Wausau

Claude and Starck

George Lougee House: 1907, Madison
Eager Free Public Library: 1908, Evansville
William Collins House: 1910, Madison
Cornelius Larson House (attributed): 1911, Madison
Columbus Public Library: 1911, Columbus
Jefferson Public Library: 1911, Jefferson
T.B. Scott Free Library: 1911, Merrill
Reedsburg Public Library: 1911, Reedsburg
Kilbourn Public Library: 1912, Wisconsin Dells
Barron Public Library: 1913, Barron
Lincoln School: 1915, Madison
Tomah Public Library: 1916, Tomah
Municipal Building and Theater: 1919, Lancaster
Baraboo High School: 1927, Baraboo

Percy Dwight Bentley

Edward Bartl House: 1910, La Crosse
Henry Salzer House: 1912, La Crosse
Chase and Wohluter Bungalows: 1912-13, La Crosse
Emil Mueller House: 1914, La Crosse
Martin Fugina House: 1916, Fountain City

Russell Barr Williamson

T. Robinson Bours House: 1921, Milwaukee
Nathan Stein House: 1921, Shorewood
Russell Barr Williamson House: 1922, Whitefish Bay
Herman Newman House: 1923, Shorewood

Robert Spencer

J.M. Sherman House: 1904, Wisconsin Dells

Glossary

Board and Batten—An interior or exterior wall covering consisting of wide boards with thin strips, or battens, used to conceal the gaps between the boards. Board and batten siding can be vertical or horizontal. One of Wright's innovations was to use it horizontally. Battens can also be used as a decorative element over Masonite or other siding, as Wright did on his Erdman prefab houses.

Cantilever—A projecting roof, balcony, or entire room supported only at one end. The other end extends outward with no visible means of support. In reality, the cantilevered portion is supported by an equal weight on the other end. Think of it as a seesaw—the part that's sticking out is supported by a counterbalancing weight.

Clerestory—A window, or row of windows, placed high on a wall just below where the wall meets the roof.

Cornice—An ornamental molding along the top of a building or wall.

Cruciform—Cross-shaped.

Gable—The triangular upper portion of a wall at the end of a pitched (sloping) roof.

Hipped roof—A roof formed by the meeting of four uniformly pitched roof surfaces. A hipped roof is pyramid-shaped.

Lintel—A piece of wood or stone that spans the top of a window or door and supports the weight above it.

Mitered joint—Formed by cutting two pieces of material at angles and fitting them together. In the 1930s, Wright began using corner windows with mitered joints. The ends of two pieces of glass were each cut at a 45 degree angle and the two pieces were glued together to form a 90 degree corner.

Molding—A continuous decorative band applied to either interior or exterior walls. Prairie School architects relied heavily on molding to produce the horizontal feel they wanted in their buildings.

Parapet—A low wall around a balcony or along the edge of a roof.

Pier—A rectangular or square, brick or stone vertical support which may stand alone or may be part of a wall.

Pilaster—A shallow pier attached to a wall.

Porte cochere—A covered entrance projecting across a driveway or entrance road so that automobiles, carriages or other vehicles may easily pass through to pick up or drop off passengers.

Roman brick—A long, thin brick often used by Prairie School architects to enhance the horizontal elements of their buildings.

Soffit—The underside of the eaves.

String Course—A continuous horizontal band of wood, stone, or brick on the exterior wall of a building.

Stucco— A type of exterior plaster made of cement, sand, lime and water, with crushed stone sometimes added for texture.

Terra cotta—A fine-grained ornamental fired clay product used for exterior decoration, or for art objects such as sculptures. It may be glazed or unglazed, molded or carved. Prairie School architects used glazed terra cotta ornament extensively.

For Further Reading

Scores of books have been written about Frank Lloyd Wright—biographies, critical analyses, reminiscences, accounts of individual buildings. Books about Prairie School architects are also beginning to appear. Here are some of the best for general readers.

The Prairie School: Frank Lloyd Wright and his Midwest Contemporaries. H. Allen Brooks. W.W. Norton & Company. An excellent account of the Prairie School, its origins, its practitioners, its demise.

Frank Lloyd Wright and the Prairie School. H. Allen Brooks. Braziller. A shorter version of Brooks' first Prairie School book. This one concentrates on photos of the buildings.

Many Masks: A Life of Frank Lloyd Wright. Brendan Gill. Ballantine Books. Biography of Wright by a reporter who knew him in the 1950s.

The Decorative Designs of Frank Lloyd Wright. David Hanks. E.P. Dutton. Excellent book about Wright's brilliance as a designer of furniture, leaded glass, and other decorative elements.

In the Nature of Materials: The Buildings of Frank Lloyd Wright 1887-1941. Henry-Russell Hitchcock. Da Capo Press. A reprint of one of the most important studies of Wright's work. A necessity if you want to study Wright seriously.

Building with Frank Lloyd Wright. Herbert and Katherine Jacobs. Southern Illinois University Press. Charming client memoir of the building of two of Wright's most famous houses.

Frank Lloyd Wright and the Johnson Wax Buildings. Jonathan Lipman. Rizzoli. Detailed account of the genesis, construction and aftermath of Wright's most famous corporate works.

Frank Lloyd Wright to 1910: The First Golden Age. Grant Manson. Van Nostrand Reinhold. An important, and very readable, book about Wright's early life and his Prairie School years. A must if you want to delve into Wright's life and work in any detail.

Frank Lloyd Wright American System Built Homes in Milwaukee. Shirley du Fresne McArthur. North Point Historical Society. Detailed but sometimes hard to follow account of Wright's early work in prefab housing. Also includes information about Russell Barr Williamson.

Frank Lloyd Wright's Usonian Houses. John Sergeant. Whitney Library of Design. Much information about Wright homes of the 1930s, 1940s, and 1950s.

Frank Lloyd Wright and Madison: Eight Decades of Artistic and Social Interaction. Edited by Paul Sprague. Elvehjem Museum of Art, University of Wisconsin-Madison. Detailed stories of the design of more than twenty-five structures for Madison, of which only eight were built.

Years with Frank Lloyd Wright: Apprentice to Genius. Edgar Tafel. Dover Publications. An engaging account of the Taliesin Fellowship in the 1930s and 1940s by one of the apprentices.

Frank Lloyd Wright: His Life and His Architecture. Robert Twombly. John Wiley & Sons. Well-written biography of Wright.

Louis Sullivan: His Life and Work. Robert Twombly. The University of Chicago Press. Very readable account of the life of this brilliant and tormented genius.

For those traveling to other states:

Wright Sites: A Guide to Frank Lloyd Wright Public Places. Edited by Arlene Sanderson. The Frank Lloyd Wright Building Conservancy. Nationwide listing of Wright structures open to the public, with tour information.

Guide to Frank Lloyd Wright and Prairie School Architecture in Oak Park. Paul Sprague. Oak Park Landmarks Commission. Five walking tours highlighting Wright's work from 1889 to 1909, as well as the works of George Maher, Robert Spencer, and local Oak Park architects who worked in the Prairie style.

The Architecture of Frank Lloyd Wright: A Complete Catalog. William Storrer. The MIT Press. Complete listing of all existing Wright structures, with a picture of each. Basic for any serious study of Wright.

The Architecture of Frank Lloyd Wright: A Guide to Extant Structures. William Storrer. WAS Productions. Maps locating every existing Wright building nationwide. Intended to be used in conjunction with the author's catalog of Wright's works.

The Prairie School in Iowa. Richard Wilson and Sidney Robinson. Iowa State University Press. The work of Wright and a number of other major and minor Prairie School architects throughout Iowa.

By Frank Lloyd Wright:

Most of Wright's writings are out of print. However, Rizzoli, in conjunction with the Frank Lloyd Wright Foundation, is beginning to reprint his works. Early books in the series will include *An Autobiography*, in which Wright tells his version of the events in his life. It is fascinating.

Index